THE DARK PEAK

and

OTHER POEMS

by

Philip Harries

Also by Philip Harries and published in the same series:

Novels
   The Pursuit of Women or Douglas Fir
   Caught in the Web

Crime Novels
   The Headhunters of St Neives
   Follow Mithras
   Beyond Calling

ISBN: 978-0-9559861-0-9

Copyright © 2008 by Philip Harries

Additional copies of this book may be purchased through Lulu Publishing at www.lulu.com/philharries

Table of Contents

The Dark Peak
At the Toad's Mouth	9
The Valley	11
In the Gorge	13
They Came for Treason	15
Can the Grass Speak?	18
Never Underestimate a Snowflake.	20
Headless Man	22
To the Quarry	25
Millstones: An Exercise in Nostalgia	26
In Padley Chapel	30
Wounded Pilgrim	31

Early Sonnets
I hardly knew my father	35
A man who has faced death	36
In Memoriam: C.G. Evans	37
She had the longest length of fetch	38
For who can say which way his mind	39
Those women who will weep	40
Who can deny the claim she made	41
It's true my hair is now more grey	42
Who dares to say?	43

Address Book	44
On Froggat Edge	45
When we abandoned the horse	46
Jubilee Hill	47

French Wedding	48
For Marcus Aurelius	54
To Miss Groby on her Retirement	54
Aubade	56
Song	56
Married Love	57
The Scene is simple	59
Don Quixote	59
From Hardwick Hall	60
To Lear with Friend	62
In Memoriam: D.K. Partridge	63
Panther	64
Brother Henry Van Hire	65
My Cat	68
Oh Dear Me!	69
When I remember Seasides	71
Lullaby	72
Incident at Carnac	73
Jane	74
On Hearing Tippet's Fourth Quartet	74

Indifferent Lights
Scratchings on the Glass:

When I was young	76
Said he.	77
On Friday, the factory where I worked	77
The household cat sits straight	77
In the heart of summer	78
In South America	80
Outside my window	80

Stained Windows
When I was young I sat in class   81
Marvel said music was mosaic   81
I took the bricks   83
The room is dim and cold   84
I am no scientist   85
Let us imagine the death   85

For Colleen   87
In Barbara Hepworth's Garden   89

From the Library at the Centre of the Universe
In The Chart Room   90
A Reading in the History Department   92
A Minute from the Horological Institute. 95
Whispering Gallery   96

Old Men Revisit   97
Shropshire Road   98
Trophy Wives   99

Sonnets of Sadness
No! I don't care   100
A pale watery gleam   101
No post again today   102
Yes, I'm an academic   103
With what steep steps   104
Yet when it came   105
No plastic smile   106

Homing   107
Walking Home   108
Thirty-Ninth Wedding Anniversary   109

The Legend of Spad

I	The Folk of the Field	111
II	A Judgement and an Execution	115
III	A Pastoral Interlude	119
IV	The Death of Owl	122
V	The Black Plague	126
VI	The Plague Continues	131
VII	And Ends	137
VIII	Aftermath	144
IX	Spad Alone	147
X	Exile	150
XI	Winter	155
XII	Partner	162
XIII	Home	165
XIV	Finale	169

Everywhere I Look   173

For Colleen

THE DARK PEAK

Meditation in a small valley
in north-east Derbyshire

AT THE TOAD'S MOUTH

For that which is honest, simple and true,
For what seems pure and uncomplicated,
For belonging
And that which sometimes we call holy,
Companionship of the most comprehensive kind,
For identity now
And now as the completion of the past,
For solace, soul's ease,
Reassurance.

Is it possible that we may return here to find such
                                                  things?
To give what little we have
And that reluctantly and by design
In order that we
Imbued with greed we may not disinherit
May yet take more than we can understand?
And will they stay our coming?

But if not otherwise then surely here,
Here beneath these sculpted rocks
Among the dark and gritty hills
Above the gently sloping moor

Where lines of darker green among the grass
Demark the drainage pattern
Where battered thorns and ragged birches
Complement the shapes of standing stones
And birds will soar on rippling wings
Along the frontier of rock and sun

Oh yes!
Here we may raise our eyes to the hills
Feel the earth solid beneath our feet
And lean against a rock and be secure
And in the evening when the setting sun
Inflames the western facing cliffs with pink,
Vermillion, gold and scarlet
And all the sky is purple
Still, transparent
We may enjoy the cusps and wisps of cloud
And gaze across the vista of the miles
With every sense disarmingly alert
And every feeling sharp.

Then may we think of gardens in the West
From which we have been long, too long excluded
Where we were happy once;
A feeling so intense
The earth stands still
The pulse stops
The sun shines but is not felt
Birds sing but cannot be appreciated

We see the past and mourn

We read the future and tremble
The present remains an ache

And all is pure illusion.

THE VALLEY

Midwinter and the armed man comes into the valley
Part warrior and part victim
But wholly pilgrim

His red shield catches and throws back
The cool heat of the sun
His visor gleams but only perhaps with frost
For his beard has thickened with ice

He leads his horse into the cold
His iron-shod feet, his horse's feet
Striking the black stones like the blows of a war
                                        hammer
The noise slides from trunk to frozen trunk
Rides up the valley sides as they climb
                              beyond him
Pauses on the sun's red reflection in the dull stream
And the black birds wheel and cry in the thin blue sky
Ravens and rooks call in the brilliant cold light
Cast shadows across the shadows of old branches
As the man plods downhill into a gloom where the
                              sun cannot reach.

After the long journey
After his seeking for what he did not know
After the long quiescent movement through the
                                        four seasons
The deliberate forgetting of the fate ahead
The increasing gripe of nightmares
And daily assumption of bravery
After the slow declension comes sudden
                                        movement
The gentle slip becomes a violent force
Here in this ordinary place
He plods weary with eyes wide from tiredness
And listens for the sound of a whetting scythe
Of a head axe

The days of warm beds and invitations
Of cosy entanglements and chivalrous charming
Will end as the Green overwhelms him
There will be no more sitting in the Great Hall
                                        with his peers
Demonstrating his courtesie and wit in the
                                        candlelight
Of sophistication and learning
Of beautiful ladies and the arts of love and war
Of resting on his laurels

We are all alone when we come to the end

IN THE GORGE

   Footprints, footprints
   How many feet have trodden here
   Even here
   Where the path descends
   Between the broken rock
   And the bounding stream?

The evidence is all around:
The stream, the rocks, the powering sun
And in the winter, snow and hail and ice
Slow as the feet
Slower than the rain and fog
Slow as the snow and hail and ice

Don't listen to the dialogue
Look at the plot

How many generations can a tree define?
Would the first users find their way as certainly
As we who climbed down yesterday?
Here, where we place our feet
Was sea, ocean, fathoms deep
And creatures moved, coiled, crawled, pounced
See! there is a sudden movement and a cloud of mud
Drifting in the tide
Wavering until disseminated

By the roots and stems of moving grasses.

Here, where we breathe
Were jungles, corals, sandbanks, hills and forests
Waving to the rhythm of the moon
While overhead
How far?
What spirit moved over the deserts of water
Urging up?
What of the creatures
Which lived among these rocks
Which sheltered in this gully
When the waves roared in
Lightning flames skipping across a black heaving
                                                            sea
Under a midnight sky
Brown waves creamed with streaming horses
Waters tearing at the fronds anchored among the
                                             crevices?
What of the crab-like creature
 Its shell split on a rock among the torrents
Or the storm-savaged vegetation
Distributed in bundles on the shore?

Oh, breathe deeply
And look up, up at the clouded sky,
Enjoy the midnight dashed with stars like sand,
Plant your feet firmly
And lean against a tree your parents knew
And look at rocks your ancestors walked round
Then close your eyes and still your beating heart.

Look at the evidence and be glad
Something of you was born and carried
Among these rocks

It survived.

Walk firmly
Unafraid
It is something to be human after all

THEY CAME FOR TREASON

Small men and virile
Wiry, with heads bald from wearing helmets
Men equipped with powerful forearms
And wrists as tough as cable
Men who have watched the world from shaded eyes
And think they have taken its measure

Who have seen the sun rise on other continents
Who have stood on bowed, sturdy legs
Their shoulders wrapped in blankets against the
                                            night
And watched the golden disc emerge
And shivered in the strangeness it revealed
As too much heat replaced extremes of cold
Explorers, they have kicked their horses on
Up dry rocky gorges where the condor floats
Adventurers, they have plodded in single file

Across the sparse plains
Where the wind always blows
And the dust was ever in their eyes and teeth

They have sweated with fever by night fires
Rolling on ledges by doubtful mountain tracks
And heard the low voices of the native creatures
As they plotted against them

They have buried their companions in shallow
                                          graves
After first appropriating their swords
Their pistols, their water-bottles
And what entitlements may have been due to them

They have watched, dry-eyed
As the smoke rose from an English auto-da-fé
And turned away without a shrug

Take what you want, said God,
But pay for it

And so it seemed inevitable,
In the fullness of time
That they should come into the government's
                                          employ
Like wandering ships to a snug anchorage

We hear them ride down Padley Gorge
Clip-clop! Clip-clop!
Their job today to take two men at prayer

Truss them like parcels
And deliver them to trial

These messengers ride easily
 Confident in the execution of their mission
A simple occupation for legitimised pirates
Perhaps they check the ropes slung from their
                                        saddles
As they talk in low voices of good times past
Of women forced and shared, of loot divided
Of how they all escaped through wit and will-power
And if by chance a star should catch their eyes
Or the angle of a rock against the sky
Should trip a memory
They will not be stirred
For rocks are rocks the whole world over
And stars can be observed from any land

Nor will they consider the noose,
Think of the knife, the hook, the axe
The hurdles or the spikes
The torn flesh, of planks slippery with blood
Of agony deliberately protracted
Inflicted by due process of the law
To reinforce the powers of a state
Which needs deaths
No - these are professional men
And lack imagination

But one small encounter
An insignificant event
In the year of the Great Armada

But the footprints will remain
As long as men and women hate oppression

The riders descend
A low laugh floats back
A snatch of dialogue in a foreign tongue

It is always the poor who suffer during change
Clip-clop! Clip-clop!

CAN THE GRASS SPEAK?

If there is one thing which is certain about grass
It is that, given an appropriate rainfall
Which can vary over an amazingly wide range
And a sufficiency of soil
Together with a suitable range of temperatures
It will grow almost anywhere

Grass is like an alternative civilisation
For it thrives and develops
Spreads in colonies
And no matter how many creatures come to eat it
It always seems to survive.

We are aware of grass as a green threat
Which makes us ambivalent in our attitude to it
We don't regard it as an enemy exactly
But rather as an intelligent and persistent barbarian

Something which needs taming
Colonising
For it is always a weed
Out of place in a flower bed
And only becomes desirable in a lawn
When it has been, as we say, cultivated

We are all imperialists when it comes to grass

By the side of the path
Encroaching on the loose stones
See
A thick brush of green spikes
Eager to grow
Desperate to populate the zone
Frantic for root space, leaf space, light space
See how proud they stand
Look how they crowd together
Making the most of what they have
Bend nearer
Look closer
Here are two blades from the same root
And see how one
In its drive upwards to the sun
Has pierced the other
Grown right through it
Split it
Killed it
Until all that is left is a brown wisp
Which the wind will soon blow away

What an interesting curiosity
Let us run our fingers through the texture
Ruffle it into place
Feel its cool, placid greenness
And go our way
Forgetting such an insignificant sight
As a matter of no importance
Or remembering it merely as an oddity

Yet on the other hand
It is a state of affairs which seems almost human

NEVER UNDERESTIMATE A SNOWFLAKE

In late autumn, after the bronze time
When the sun pales and the valley cools
The rocks chill for lack of stimulus
The stream flows to a lighter, different sound
Mist lingers under the branches and leaves of the
                                                gorge
Earth stamps hard as iron

Later, from heavy grey clouds
From low clouds drifting from the west
Comes the first snow of the ageing year
It will, perhaps, be gentle on this occasion
Subtle and insinuating
Falling, it seems, without weight

And reluctant to find a solid resting place

From this dancing activity of the middle air
Too hectic to be distinguished
Will come a new order
Temporary and strangely beautiful
For there will come a time when the last flake will
                                                            fall
Though it will be impossible to demonstrate which
                                                            one
And the sun will shine in the woods and dazzle the
                                                            eyes
The sky will be blue and the snow level and smooth
The stream will run gently between white banks
The trees will be black in the sunlight
And throw blue shadows across the white hills

There will be a pause while all the vale recovers
Assimilates, comes to terms, adjusts to the new
                                                          situation
Draws unsteady, excited breaths
And then there will be movement
Cautious and unprepared at first
A bird will call harshly and fly a branch
In a glittering shower of snow
A squirrel will hop hesitantly round the bole of a
                                                               tree
Trying to recall a topography now muffled

Then
 From across the steep valley

Echoing briefly down the shaded gorge
The sound of a branch snapping
Will startle through the thin air
There will be a silence of intense listening
Following the short explosion
Some birds will rise, unsettled
And the squirrel may pause in the act of peeling a
                                                          nut
Ears pricked, nose twitching, eyes glaring
But the moment will pass
The echoes will fade among the upper trees
Silence and furtive activity will resume
Leaving only the questions

For who can say how long
How many years the branch had been dying?
Who can say when it began
In the time of which generation?
And who can compute which snowflake
By what circumstance of drift
By which addition of weight
At what precise time
Caused the fracture?

When the axe falls too gently and the neck is
                                            not parted
The shock my well be intolerable
When the journey's end is reached
Whatever has been discovered
Must be accepted

However unexpected it may be
When the event comes
As it will come in its own time
According to a timetable of its own making
In a timescale of its own construction
The moment will change all
Is irrevocable and not permanent
However it may seem to the contrary

In this lies the strength of the snowflake

HEADLESS MAN

His huge figure dominates the clearing
Ancient and timeless
Compiled from many memories
Built from conflicting fictions
But real nevertheless
So that he is both frightening and intimate
Instinctively so

See him sitting on a boulder
Dappled by sunshine
Surrounded by the brown leaves of last autumn
Unmoving
Deckled with reddish brown leaves
And mottled with shafts of silver light
A theatrical effect created by the mind
And imposed on imagined reality

The place is silent

Like a pre-Raphaelite picture
Despite the detail of his clothes
The stitches in his surcoat
The rivets and dull green gleam of his armour
The individuality of each green lock of hair
The bulge of the green muscles in the green hose
The delicate puckering of the green lips
The green veins on the slack hands
Swelling with the green blood beneath the green
                                              skin
The sideways glance from the green eyes
Full of far-away sadness

What stays is a knowledge of intelligence
Which was more than adequate at the time
That and a similar feeling of nostalgia
And a willingness to overlook certain boisterous
                                                brutalities
Until we see the battleaxe propped against a boulder
And detect a red edging to the green blade

It is important to consider what could have
                                                happened
And the implications of victory
And be glad
As well as spare more than an inward tear for the
                                                loser
For he too is part of our apprehension
And must be continuously defeated

Yet love and accept him

TO THE QUARRY

When we follow a path to the place where the way
                                                    divides
And both new tracks seem to go in the right
                                                    direction
There always follows a difficult matter of choice
Together with the possibility of being wrong
Of running off in some new, uncalculated direction
Of coming to a dead end
Of finishing in a difficult piece of country
And having to retrace our steps
While we regret the waste of time or the dashed
                                                    hopes
Even, in extreme cases, the damage
Which seems permanent at the time

So shall we take the one which seems the more
                                                    direct
And follow as it narrows to the horizon?
Or shall we meander enticingly with the other
And follow the river as it winds and leaps?
Ducking under low-swinging branches
Stepping and striding over the glistening humps of
                                                    roots
Listening to the music of the water
Inhaling the smell of the stream to the exclusion of all
                                                    else
Hypnotised almost
Concentrated certainly in the small world
Of leaf and branch and rock and damp earth

So that where we are going recedes to the back of
                                            our minds
And we only know the travelling is all
And reason enough for the journey?

The straight path leads to the quarry
And a dead end

MILLSTONES: AN EXERCISE IN NOSTALGIA

I first came here some fifty years ago
When I and all the world were young
And full of hope
When no achievement seemed impossible
For we breathed a richer, sweeter air
And happiness was something of a right

But now how different it all appears
Now that a deeper music underwrites my thoughts
And I see disillusion here
The ruins of a once good enterprise

And yet my memory tells me true
That nothing here has changed intrinsically
The quarry is no smaller than it was
And no more dissipated
Millstones still stand in rank to be collected
As once they did - how many years before?
Two hundred? Maybe more

From here they should have gone to grind the corn
At Sacrewell in Cambridgeshire
To the Blackwater mills in Ireland
To all the little settlements where water eased the
                                            shoulder
Where factors were reflected in deep pools
And bubbled with the joy of craftsmanship

But here they stand abandoned
Unwanted
 Sinking immutably into the earth
Tombstones of their own departure
Spattered with green waterstains of lichen
And in the rocks around are those half-shaped
And some marked out and never cut
When overnight the trade was killed

The grass returned
Trees took purchase once again
Sift crept across the rutted trail
And partly levelled
There was a time when once I took this as a fact
And little more than that
For we must have change
Change is a sign of life

This change led to a death

The air is humid here as befits a tomb
Still, with no insect murmur
Quiet, with no river noise

Warm with the warmth of the rocks
Only the roots move and the grass rustles
The leaves unfurl, crisp and fall
The stones melt invisibly
Slower than my seventy years
Slower than my lifetime
More gradually than a hundred generations
Outlasting the acorn and the beechmast
But imperceptively and unalterably shedding
Skinning

This is what we call stability
Mind recognises that
But Mind seeks change
Mind needs change

Mind both bore and killed this place
And gave it neither funeral nor help
Mind colonises the world like grass
And battles with itself like roots

The weak and the poor always suffer from Mind
Because it can take no responsibility
Once this valley was filled with noise
Of mallets driving wedges
Of chisels shaping and dressing
Of the rattle of tackle and the creak of wagons
The impatient snorting of a team of horses
Jingling brasses and stamping feet
As another load is packed in straw

A scene fit for a jig-saw puzzle or a calendar
And yet - who knows?
There might have been a cheerful whistle
From some contented mason.
Such things are not recorded in the rocks
Mind deals in facts and that is only an illusion
At best a fancy
At worst a soft-centred whimsy
Glamourising the past

No - the place had to die
And it died
Dropped from an indifferent mouth
And left to rot

Why should I waste my time
 Shaking my fist at the past?

And yet
And yet
There is a sadness in this nook
Which qualifies its beauty

I sometimes think my youth died here

IN PADLEY CHAPEL

Here
Now
Today
Remain within this bare room
And let the stillness invade your senses
Allow the silence to supersede your wishes
Permit the spirit to overwhelm your perceptions
For the air is sweeter here
An essence requiring submission
With the compelling gentleness of a flowing tide
You will not see visions
You will see white-washed walls
Rough beams supporting an ancient roof
A wrought-iron cross and thin candles and small
                                      windows
There will be a feeling of inwardness
Not claustrophobia but concentration
And evidence of past and continuing piety.

There have been pilgrims here
Who have receded to unmarked graves
Who are remembered only by their mite of good
Contributed to the general store and accounted
                                        here
Each, for one instant. seizing a glimpse of eternity
As a reward

WOUNDED PILGRIM

Waiting

Under the floor of Padley Chapel
Beneath the concrete of the tower block
Living in the clay below the motorway junction

Waiting

Under the gothic cathedral and the village hall
Beneath the palaces and municipal offices
Below the city and great financial houses

Waiting

Under the concrete aprons of international airports
Beneath the missile silos and nuclear fall-out shelters
Below the factories, the railway stations,
The monuments to heroes and victory

Waiting
Dormant seeds and sleeping roots

Let the climate alter but a small degree
And the glaciers will return
The golden eagle will survey the new snowfields
From his eyrie
A desert of reality will crawl across the landscape

Romanticism is a disease of the temperate zones

Consider Mind and its struggle with the world
The desire of Mind to conquer the world
To name, weigh, measure, delineate, alter
And thus to tame, to civilise
To cultivate

After the thought comes the action
Comes the deed, comes the change
Comes the indifference

The seeds are sleeping
The roots are lying in wait

Mind surveys, owns, formulates, dispenses

Waiting

Consider the slow civil war which is a human
                                                being
And consider the consequences if one should win
If the burden should be permanently lifted
By the victory of one side or the other

Waiting

Study that bird
See how well it flies
How it floats through the air, twisting and turning
Rippling and constantly adjusting the subtle
                                                feathers
As it glides along the edge

Do we wonder as we plant our feet on the ground
And lean against a convenient tree
Are we at home down here as he up there?

For times come when the burden is intolerable
When we envy the mastery of the eagle
The slow growing wisdom of a tree
The seeming serenity of gently blowing moorlands
The placid assertion of self contained in a rocky feature
We are forever on the threshold
Afraid to leave the dark and yet afraid to go back
Nervous of the light and yet attracted to it
Always waiting
Burdened with waiting and the knowledge of conflict
Seeking for a certainty which will not betray us
Needing an authority we cannot deny
Yet heartsore with demands
Soul weary
Never at home anywhere

Yet in the Chapel
Or in the small rocky nook which was a quarry once
We may for a moment lay our burden down
We may forget self and discover reconciliation
And through the process of forgetting find an entity
To which we may submit if only for a moment
That there may come a peace to all warring factions
And through this moment of understanding

We may learn to love the opposites by knowing
                                                       them
And accept them for their disparate, discordant
                                                  activities

Do not tamper with the text

At the time when the day has not yet faded into
                                                   evening
When the stars are bright but the sun has not yet
                                               disappeared
When all is balanced between two lights
When leaves are still and birds are silent, listening,
The time which sometimes we consider holy,
The wounded pilgrim limps into the valley
He cannot tell whether the path he walks is the
                                                right one
He does not know whether the imperfect vision
                                                he clutches
Contains his own illusion of reality
He only knows he must progress
Limp on
Shamble into a run
Halt to ease his hurts
Before hope drives him on once more
To pluck simplicity from complication
Rest from eternal movement
To abstract love from competition
And listen to a single melody among the world's
                                                discord

EARLY SONNETS

(1)

I hardly knew my father, never knew
The sweet and secret ecstasy of coping,
By proxy as it were, with all the hue
And cry of life; I never saw him loping
With certain steps among the undergrowth
Which trips a father's feet; I never heard
His explanations of the snags of youth,
Nor can remember any tender word.
And so, a father now, I have no guide
To follow through the maze of parenthood;
My pattern is pragmatically tied,
My pain is in the doubt of doing good.
But when I do not know which way to turn
I use his only gift, the will to learn

(2)

A man who has faced death remains afraid:
He knows too well each coaxing, friendly feature;
The smile that comforts while his memories fade
And turns him to a love-less, lonely creature.
His life has taken on a new dimension,
It has a depth he never guessed before;
Each action seems to have a new intention
Each thought an extra unsought either-or.
So love and friendship clash in competition,
And life and death are real alternatives;
The fact is there with or without volition -
He must preserve the balance while he lives.
He fears the tempting voice which tells his end:
True courage lays his life down for a friend.

(3)

IN MEMORIUM: C. G. EVANS

So much vitality! And is it all
Gone under the hill? Is nothing left behind
Of herself? When she heard the final call,
Did she answer it with her usual blind
Response; throw off, like bedclothes, all her head
Contained, the wisdom of her heart, the love
Of friends and pupils, leaping without dread
From this cold world, a sweet and fiery dove?
Ah no! It is impossible that she,
Who loved her life, was gentle and adept,
Should love death too! It is as thief that we
Condemn him now: he stole her while she slept.
For he came quiet as though he were aware
A cruel, clumsy move would startle her.

(4)

She had the longest length of fetch I've seen
And pulled men's heads from what was in their
                                            minds;
She made the married think what might have been
Had they their youth and all the force which binds;
The single - well - the single merely gaped
At what their brains refused to see as true,
And consequently she progressed unraped
In thought and fact, the leader of the queue.
Her mind was pure of any wicked thought,
No single taint or stain lay on her life,
Her bosom and her thighs were richly wrought
And yet no man had needed her for wife.
And so for me she will remain the proof
Strong cloth requires a warp as well as woof.

(5)

For who can say which way his mind should turn?
Towards the light or dark? He knows the dark,
A fearful, friendly, gloomy, fertile place,
Of shapes and thoughts; where horrors make their mark
Indelibly, upon his learning soul;
Where battles fought and won, or, darkly, lost,
Are all pure gain despite their nervous toll;
The place he takes his risks and pays the cost.
The incandescent glare of light he knows,
Which dries the plant while yet it makes it grow,
That sucks the colour from the blazing rose,
That stimulates and kills all by its blow.
Between these two the sane man pegs his knife:
A little madness oils the wheels of life.

(6)

Those women who will weep their way to power
Enforcing all in floods of self-attention -
The female over-rank in sweet and sour,
The masculine control in self-contention
And both exhaust in irrigant excess -
Are liberators of their own pure souls;
In innocence is found their real success,
Impression is their first and last of goals.
A mirror is the mark of suave self-knowing,
We peer and pose before a naive glass;
If what we see will set our eyes a-flowing,
The fault is ours, we should not be so crass.
Our image is the glint in other eyes;
Reflection should not cause the tears to rise.

(7)

Who can deny the claim she made her mind?
Her parents had no dealing in her growth;
It's true they did not mean to be unkind -
She had her life and they their marriage oath -
No child they'd wanted to disturb the pattern
Of loving fostered to a grand obsession;
The babe that came, they took pains, would not batten
Upon each other's dearest sole possession.
And so, outside the furnace door she lingered,
An alien, knee-deep in her neglect;
She guessed what love was, but she never fingered
Experiences that cherish and project.
A single view of love has made her blind -
Who can deny her claim she made her mind?

(8)

It's true my hair is now more grey than black,
And I am slower than I used to be,
And what was tight is sometimes rather slack
And quieter than it was; this I'll agree!
I've wrinkles now where once my face was
                                          smooth,
My joints will creak if they are stressed too much,
But what was once undisciplined is couth;
Contentment suits me better than all such!
Time takes and gives with unremitting haste,
Each year I live is loss and gain combined,
What once was fire and dross has been replaced
By contemplation ever unconfined,
Yet when I see your smile, I say, in truth,
You give to age the imagery of youth.

(9)

Who dares to say I've seen my better times?
I will deny the sad truth of the phrase;
The things that I do now are not just mimes
Of what I once did in my younger days:
Perhaps less often, but more deeply felt,
And yet more fitted to the spread of life,
My actions are the product of the melt
Of youth and time and intellectual strife -
Or so, in pride, I claim. And yet, I muse,
Did I, along the path which I have passed,
Choose right, or even have the right to choose?
What shaped the shoe - the hammer or the last?
It's strangely comforting when I remember
The chill beneath the gold in each September.

ADDRESS BOOK

Cold winter sunlight floods the room. I sit,
Unwilling, to complete the annual task,
Address book open, of sending Christmas
Greetings to my friends, and those who claim
My friendship: colleagues, people I met once
On holiday and quite forgotten 'til
Their cards land grinning on the front door mat.

At my elbow lies my mother's book, faded,
Red, bound with a thick elastic band;
The names it holds go back for fifty years
Or even more. All are now crossed out
Save one or two, one sister's and her children.
Many are names that punctuate my childhood
Like commas in a dream. I see again
A pair of spectacles, fading kindly eyes,
Smell lavender and hear the creak of moving
Corsetry. 1 remember husbands,
Dapper, hearty, each with his small moustache,
Punching the air with his cigarette,
Or talking with it slanting in his mouth
Just like the Prince of Wales
Before the great betrayal.
                        And mother,
Coming from the kitchen like a train
From a tunnel, wreathed in smiles and wisps
Of steam, to place a bowl of white potatoes
On its mat, before sending me to bed.

All gone, they must have gone, for they were old
When I was young. Indeed, the evidence
Is here, in mother's crossings-out.

My nib has dried. It scratches, splutters,
Scrawls.
The job must be done:
Who knows how many pens are lifted,
Ready to scratch my name?
The sun goes in. I choose another card.

ON FROGGAT EDGE

The morning sun contains a touch of gold;
The air is still;
Sounds echo sharply from the hill;
Birdsong quickens in the early blaze;
The crumbling walls enfold
A maze of paths, unrolled
Between the husk of slowly melting haze.

A moment, this, of solemn, silent mirth;
Then trees are glossed
With traces of dissolving frost;
The power grows in striking fashion;
Experience of the earth,
Of growth, decay, rebirth
Is captured, lost, within a moment's passion.

Buds open slowly in the strengthening heat;
A wayward ant
Runs neatly up a ripening plant;
Transparency of day must now suffice;
The placid hills repeat
That life is incomplete -
Natura naturans in paradise!

WHEN WE ABANDONED THE HORSE

When we abandoned the horse
And took to the car
We lost the rhythm of our countryside.
Our life lost all its subtle syncopations.
Our music, now, reciprocates
On two, four, or eight cylinders,
Or tries to exist in no time,
(An abstraction that is palpably absurd).
We have lost our allegri and andanti:
What is life without non piu lento?
Or vivace without non senza grave?
But worst of all
We have lost con amore

JUBILEE HILL

Yes, I was there that night. I saw
The fire lit, the gorgeous flames draw
High, like twisting hands in prayer;
Saw faces streaked with light, the stare
Of eyes, caught, passive with desire.

Behind me, in the living dark,
Sad fetches watched each dying spark
And sighed; I felt their presence near
And for a heart beat I was freer:
Time leapt into a point of fire.

Spirits mustered on that bony hill,
Come to the Celebration! Still,
Quiet, grave, like stirring embers,
Paid their tribute as past members
In the community of flames.

'God save !' the cry went up. And yet
God save who? What ritual debt
Was being honoured? What old blight
Averted; prayer granted? That night
It was a queen the crowd acclaims.

FRENCH WEDDING

It was a strange holiday in the end -

We had no plan when we arrived in France,
Had thought to tour in our secular English manner,
Had thrown the car over the Channel,
Had followed its nose in our pragmatic English
                                          way,
Drifting rather than driving,
Our half-dreamed purpose to enjoy the sun,
The sense of space, the different style,
The freedom of a land which spreads for miles,
Its ripening fields and poppies in the corn,
With vines and apples climbing, fruiting free;
To ponder, in our dim sundrunken haze,
The huge cathedrals and ancient battlefields,
The forests and the land which no one used,
And spawned the dream which every tourist has
Of dropping anchor somewhere here,
For here, it seemed, we could be free,
With empty roads and wide unbroken skies,
Small market towns, cheap wine, fresh food,
The sweet and midnight peace of starlit nights.

Oh no, there was no purpose, no pattern,
Mere tourism,
Serendipity,
Hedonism,

Dropping of all critical faculties,
Recreation,
And if anything else happened it would be a bonus!
And in this mood we squandered in the valley of the
                                  Rhine
Alsace,
And browsed through smaller, friendlier towns,
Colmar, Obernei -
Drank wine and wandered cobbled streets
Beneath laden, scented window boxes,
Admired the wooden houses and their carving,
And then we raised our eyes towards the hills,
And next day climbed up to the famous citadel,
The Church and Nunnery of Ste Odile,
A star no tourist could ignore
And just the sort of place we'd come to visit.

And so we walked its shady grounds
Below the massive walls,
Marched the Stations of the Cross
And found the tumbled, earthed-up pagan walls,
And came back to the courtyard and the car.

But first an ice cream and a drink.

And then we saw a line of cars outside the
                                  Convent gate,
Doors open in the heat,
The passengers spilled out, seeking shade under
                                  the trees.
A wedding!

What simple fun to sit and watch it happen,
Eat an ice cream and watch it like urchins.
We wouldn't do it at home!

There is the Bride's father in the tight black suit
Tugging at his tie and wiping at his neck,
Plump and red and wet,
Small and oddly triumphant;
Perhaps his daughter has made a good match?
One away from the few hectares of salad greens,
The two precious vines, the part-time husbandry,
To one who is looking for strength, endurance,
                                    meekness?
And that must be her mother,
The one in the inappropriate floppy pastel shades,
Who seems too heavy for her shoes;
The one in tears who leans, hanky in hand
On any female shoulder she can find;
Surely she is gaining a son
Not losing a daughter?

And those, perhaps, must be her brothers,
The two in the shiny blue suits,
Red socks and brown shoes,
Dark slicked-back hair;
They look awkward and embarrassed.
Never mind, they will get drunk afterwards
And disgrace themselves at the reception,
Just like younger brothers at home

And all the others, obviously relatives
And friends
And friends of friends:
How smart they all look in their finery!

And now here comes the Bride.
Her car stops and she is helped out:
A shimmering vision of white,
Veiled and surrounded by little girls in white
Who pull and push and pat her dress,
Plumping it into shape.

The men come to attention:
Cigarettes are stamped out
And the smoke waved away,
Jackets are tugged straight
And mirrored hair polished once again.

There is an arch through into the Convent
Where tourists cannot go.
The huge gates open, leading to the Church:
The procession moves off towards the opening:
A grey old nun appears in the gloom
To meet and welcome them,
To bless and lead them in.

Then the gates close with a bang
And I am reminded of the children of Hamelin
Gone into the hillside,
For I feel a sense of loss and anticlimax.

That seems to conclude the entertainment.
The chauffeurs are sitting on the grass:
One is drinking red wine from a bottle;
He wipes the neck and passes it on.
It seems very calm and normal
Except for the sense of loss

No - not loss:
A sense of something not normal,
Not English;
Something wrong by English standards.

Where is the Bridegroom?

And then realisation came,
Cold in that heat,
With a trickle down the spine
And a closing of the eyes against the truth.

The Bride was, to be honest, quite old:
The father was pleased:
The mother sad:
The brothers awkward and uncomfortable,
The rest embarrassed,
Making the best of it,
Looking sideways to see what the rest of us
                                        thought:
Only the chauffeurs were unconcerned.

There is no Bridegroom!
Or rather, to put it another way,

He is all around us,
If you hold to that sort of thing.

Oh, our dissenting souls!
How shocked they were!
How quickly we packed and left!

And yet, as we drove down the hill to the plain of
                                      the Rhine
We remembered the Bride's face:
Radiant,
Certain,
Looking inwards with a little smile of expectation,
A being already apart.
And we wished her a proper wedding,
A blissful consummation,
A happy marriage,
And left the place as fast as we decently could
And thought of England.

We could do no more than that.

FOR MARCUS AURELIUS

Thoughts felt; sensations veined and dark,
Crimson, circling; steady beating climate,
Warm, domestic; no other known and yet
Knowledge now I am myself my ark.
Then world contracts, expels to noise, cold, dawn
Of public weather; outside, other, worse!
Inconsequentiality! The hearse
Is manufacturing on which all must be borne.
Crawl, stand, walk where? Driven by that first
                                                blow
In vain steps, pick best from worst, seek joy
In declination. Make comfort where I can
Is fruitless, passive: all is go
To further down. Clear eyes alone deploy
What strength is left to making of a man.

TO MISS GROBY - ON HER RETIREMENT

    What will happen to your knowledge
    Now your teaching days are done?
    Will you leave it on your bookcase
    As you search for endless fun?
    Is it lumber in your attic?
    Is it jumble, now, for sale?
    Will you use it up in crosswords
    Or just hang it on a nail?

The store you had seemed endless,
Cyclopaedic in its scope,
Will it help you now - forgive me -
When your life seems short on hope?
Will it help to eke your pension,
Will it guide you when you shop,
Putting salt upon your lettuce
And mustard on your chop?

And when a rainbow spreads itself
And hangs suspended there,
Will your knowledge of the spectrum
Keep the edge from your despair?
When you're waiting at a bus stop
And the rain drips from the trees,
Will your knowledge of bone structure
Ease the aching in your knees?

However will you pass the time
With none to educate?
Will your knowledge of the poets
Reconcile you to your fate?
Do you question, in your silence,
As around your mind you roam,
Was the journey worth the making
And is where you've got to, home?

AUBADE

How sweet it is to draw a deep
Unquavering and reassuring breath;
To see a yearling apple tree
Sport a ring of blossom at her throat;
To smell the damp earth drying in the sun;
To watch the cherry flowers as they fall
And hear a blackbird whistling on the roof.

SONG

Who am I to ask for pleasure?
Should I not accept content,
Useful work, creative leisure
And time to repent?
Happiness is summer lightning
Joining earth and firmament.
  This I know
O this, O this, O this I know.

Who am I to run from sadness?
Should I not accept my lot?
Humanity denied breeds madness,
Air and earth forgot.
Sadness is my brother's shadow,
Blackest when the sun is hot.
  This I know
O this, O this, O this I know.

Every joy is lined with sorrow,
Every man is clay and sir,
So, Lady, make your task to borrow
Happiness from care.
We're the dreams of ancient atoms,
Ecstasy's a fitful flare.
      This I know
      This, O this
O this, I truly, truly know!

MARRIED LOVE

Today, I want to give a toast
To married love;
A celebration
Of occasional ecstasy.

For when 1 think
Of all the obstacles in our way
It becomes a minor miracle;
Children most of all -
Coming in too late or too early,
Being too noisy or too quiet,
Sitting in the dark in the front room
Or in the light in the kitchen -
What are they up to?

And then all the other things -
Dust on the dressing-table,
Clearing up after supper,

Worrying about our son
Who is in Birmingham and on the dole,
And whether the neighbours can hear us
(Even though we never hear them)
And whether the taps are dripping
And the plug unplugged on the television
And whether the window is closed
Or open
And worrying because we can't find
Anything to worry about

So I sit in bed
And raise my morning cup of tea
In salute
And you ask me what I'm laughing at
And when I say
It is a toast. a celebration, gratitude
You say no
It is thankfulness
And I think about it for a moment
And agree
After all, the best part of married love
Is that there is always tomorrow night
Or even next week
For where there is love
There is always hope.

THE SCENE IS SIMPLE

The scene is simple, windswept, bare and bleak:
A naked birch half-beaten to the ground
Across a weather-splintered rock; and all
Around, the sour plateau of the moor.
If I should axe the tree, what voice would speak
In outrage? Roll away the stone, what sound
Of' protest? Or fire the ling, what could call
Me scourge? To be is only to endure.
But if I take the tree and shape it, make
A pipe or fiddle; if I could awake,
By chipping at the rock, a note that I
Call true; or, in paint, revivify
The blaze - whose view? What music? Whose new
                                              voice?
And if I did, what reason to rejoice?

DON QUIXOTE

As a fold or crinkle in magnetic tape
Will slow down the melody
Or interrupt the rhythm
And break the concentration of our listening
Concealing the pattern of the music from us
Or revealing a pattern that we did not think it had
Bringing a moment of pain or exasperation,
So does a wrinkle in the spread of time
Exasperate us with its evidence of painful moments;

The structure, the pattern, is not as we believed
And our acceptance is expelled
By something altogether more frightening -
An exceptional circumstance
An extreme case:
A man trapped in a bubble of pain
Broken on a wheel we did not know existed
Turned on a lathe we thought imaginary
Burned in a fire we thought extinct
Hated by a God we thought long superseded
Interrupts the flow of our minds
And opens a door we had rather remain closed.

FROM HARDWICK HALL

There was no plan: no genius laid down
What shape this open countryside should take;
The plough was laid to ground, axe to the tree,
Scythe to the grass and sickle to the wheat,
Brick placed on brick, track beaten into path
And into lane, sour land refreshed, sweet water
Ducted, fields captured from the common land,
Houses raised and children reared, barns and
                            churches
Placed where custom, ease, convenience for work
Will make them look what we call beautiful.

Here, sitting on this bridge, I can descry
The whole, regard this now as product

Of that past, for what is now. but past
Revitalised and turned to our advantage?
The countryside contains it all: history
Stitched into the weaving of a haystack,
A battle celebrated in a clump of trees,
Old towns revealed in slowly ripening corn,
Ambition in the turning of a vane,
All past subsumed and used, moving
Ever forward, until this now, in turn,
Is made new growth.

Yet up here, in the palace on the hill,
Process is frozen, senses are confused.
Now and then permute to then and now,
But always then in now.
Purpose is gone;
Influence, power, vanished with the years,
Drained into fields and woods, the borrowed
                              strength poured back.
Life is gone, sunk into the ground.

Here, sitting on the bridge, I can descry
The whole in moments, possibly predict
The near past from the further, the first past
From the then.
There are two nows
And the price of the one is always the other.

TO LEAR WITH FRIEND

It was all new to him
Ripeness and howl and never
Skipping King
Gimlet questions
Stumbling earl
Blindness
Love and reconciliation
Hatred, ambition, death
All the large concerns,
Of warring natures

He is well-to-do also
With a daughter whom he loves..
I watched him watching
Him enthralled
Me smug

It was all daughters for him

What's real resides in what's particular
Which humbled me

IN MEMORIUM: D. K. Partridge

In this corner of a draughty island
Beneath the wind-scraped sky
Forsythia is blowing merrily
Daffodils flounce in gay impetuosity
Only the solemn hyacinth stands attentive
As she who loved flowers
Passes through her garden

She leaves the sons and grandsons,
The daughters and great-grand daughters
Of her skill in propagation
She leaves these blooms
Unacknowledged, unacknowledging,
Her only heirs

The full garden, the empty house
An allegory she would have liked,
Accepting the grimness
And relishing the opposition

PANTHER

The panther stirred
Moved
Cleared his throat beguilingly
And spoke

Always and always and always
In the streets of your towns
You will think you see my shape;
On the village greens, over the habitable hills,
In the high cold places,
Across the hot wet places,
Throughout all torrid, temperate and arctic zones
You will just fail to see me pass.

When two or three are gathered in friendly conversation
My shadow makes the gathering complete;

When you draw your curtains in the evening
At the corner of your eye you will think you
                                        see me
Slide into the deeper shadows of the dusk,
And in the morning you will be too late
To see my spoor imprinted in the dew.

In the eyes of the ones you love
Even in most intimate moments
You will see the thought behind my eyes

Behind their eyes
And the thought behind their eyes
Will be found among the thoughts behind your eyes
Leaving no mark for the senses to perceive.

I clear the river like a leaping bridge
And give it definition and perspective
In the depths of mind
In the well of memory.

BROTHER HENRY VAN HIRE WILL NOW EXPLAIN TO US EXACTLY WHAT HAPPENED IN HAYWOOD CAR PARK WHEN WE THOUGHT HE WAS SUFFERING FROM TOO MUCH OF EXCESS - HENRY?

That time, the summer of the blistering drought,
My wife and I, tormented by the heat,
Like many others, found ourselves forced out
By petrol fumes and stink of city street.

We went in search of air that's fit to smell,
To try and gain our mental equipoise,
And came here, to the Country, where the spell
Of Nature brings her own sweet healing joys.

We chose to park the car just over there,
Among the bushes, there, in that green bay;
A quiet, private situation, where
We could relax our tensions through the day.

Susan was tired. She let her head go back
And dozed. My paper on the wheel I spread,
Wound down my window just the veriest crack
To let my pipe smoke filter out, and read.

How long we stayed there, tranquil, I don't know;
The heat grew hotter as the peaceful day
Passed us by, until the gentle shadow
On my paper eased its benison away.

Among those bushes, in the birch tree's shade,
Where all the air a solemn silence holds;
Where all of Nature seems this one small glade;
Where comes the Native Spirit which enfolds
My own; where all the leaves are still and thick
With heat; - something is unnaturally wrong!
And in a moment, I am feeling sick
With fear - the birds had ceased their ceaseless
                              song!

Let not the Cynic mock! That's how it took
Me! A fertile incandescent terror rode
Triumphantly through every glade and nook
Of my poor body! Each and every lode
Of bone was - I'd take almost any oath! -
Transformed to jelly! It was living death

Of sorts - imposed paralysis of sloth!
And then amidst my sobs, I caught my breath -
I heard a footfall in the undergrowth!

The footsteps stopped! My breathing almost stopped
Too! And then his face came into view: -
Two slanting eyes; red full lips; an uncropped
Beard; a hooked nose thrusting proudly; two
Slanting eyebrows, pointing upwards to a pair
Of little goat horns; dark amber glowing
Eyes, inspecting me, and, most hard to bear,
The red lips curved in laughter, mocking, knowing!

And in that moment when I met his eyes
It seemed as though my sanity was burned
Under a merciless sun, frozen under skies
Of winter: - ploughed, harrowed, reaped - and
                                        spurned!

One instant only! Then his gaze withdrew;
His life ebbed from me as he set me free:
His presence faded like the summer dew
And left the car to Susan and to me.

And that was it! And then I heard the thrill
Of birds again; a whisper in the tree;
The hum of insects, and, fading on the hill,
The lingering echo of a melody.

And yet I loved him, pagan, solitary!
His lonely piping from oblivion
Stirred yearning echoes in my memory
And started dreams of happiness long gone.

Yes, ordinary Nature crowded in:
I merely watch the scene: 1 cannot greet
Fish, flesh or fowl or tree as friend or kin;
The elegy was mine, for I am incomplete.

MY CAT

With what Passion, when we meet,
Do we one another greet!
First he purrs and thrusts his jaws
On to mine and plucks his paws
Or, whiskers forward, licks my nose
And blinks his eyes as kinship grows.
Eye to eye and face to face
That's how predators embrace.

Then he lies upon my knees,
Stretches out and takes his ease,
Lifts his head and pricks his ears,
Sings his song to calm my fears,
Rolls and squirms upon his side
And once again rejoins my pride.
That's the way things tend to be
When two predators agree.

On his back, on the mat -
What a sweet domestic cat!
See, his fur is soft and warm,
Whoever could he hurt or harm?
Quite unconscious in the heat,
Who could fear his gentle feet?
And yet I know, my furry friend,
For you to live, another life must end.

OH DEAR ME!
A TIRADE ON THE SHORE AT AMROTH

Although my anger's gone and my wild outrage
Turned to laughter, the bruises stay. They ripen
Over time like dropped fruit and I am tender
On the subject still. Oh, I was hurt!
Not in my body - that would have healed by now -
But in my mind. My brain has been abused,
My pride offended, my common sense snubbed
And critical faculty ignored,
Undercut, reduced to nothing, jilted!
And I was treated like a stupid stump,
Six foot of timber stranded in the sand,
An object merely, without eyes or voice
But all ears! A something that an idiot
Might think was lower than himself and so
Decide to educate and enlighten,
Show the true path, engineer in logic -
Oh, I have heard of instruments of pain,
Engines for torture, but believe me now

I have never met such torment as he
Dished out! Seven projects all dissected
And put back in such detail would corrode
A saint! In language of such even, calm
Contempt, such higher intellectual
Conceit, such vacuous banality,
Such excellence of common-place resort!
Oh no! Am I an infant now to learn
How to weigh and measure and in a while
Divide and multiply? For that's the sum
Of all that he can do. Arithmetic!
Not even Maths, but simple computation,
Not even thought, but reason's step-child, guess,
Or by a process of elimination -

And while he talked, the tide came in and went,
I watched a sea-bird soaring near the sun,
A crab ran sideways, splashed into a pool,
The wet sand bubbled full of generous life,
The earth performed her ceremonial turn -
All movements natural and curved and live,
While he trudged
Across the arid desert of his mind
In one straight line - no allowed diversions -
Inflexibly towards the far horizon.
I swear that while he talked I heard the wheels
Within his head whirr, the cogs clank,
The little hammers striking in his brain,
The spring creak, the escapement - Ha! what
          chance
For me of running from his mechanical

Perceptions? And here's the worst! I've caught the
                                                          plague!
The man has left me ticking like a clock!

WHEN I REMEMBER SEASIDES

When I remember seasides, I don't see
The tourists' havens - cream teas, fish and chips
Accents and brassware, plates and boats and sails,
Unlikely yachting caps and silly girls,
And thin young men with nothing in their faces
And only energy to spend, or old
Rich men with bronzed young wives, awaiting
Widlowland with sly impatience -
And then
The sharks, bigger than any fish which swim
The sea - men with smooth, shiny faces
And smooth shiny cars, who would turn the place
They have just bought into the thing just left.
Importing their frustration with their cash.
Nor do I see the history of the place,
Glorious though that be, for most of it
Was made by people acting contrary
To life, men like Arthur, shepherd or farmer,
Desperately slashing with a pike,
His red face streaming sweat in the torchlight
And feeling sorry for the men he hurts;
Or a group of men plotting treason,
Or palely dying because they worship God

In the wrong way according to the state.
And then I see the fort at the harbour's mouth –
                              ruined!
Which makes me feel more cheerful at once
Because if such a thing that's built to last
Can in so short a time come tumbling down,
How short a span can be afforded to
These rich men's boxes, bingo halls and clubs?
They could be swept away like last year's fashion.
In fifty years there might be nothing left
But fields and trees, the farmers at their work,
The harbour and the little fishing boats,
The cleansing tides, the healing sun and moon.

Too much to hope for? Think of Stonehenge now.

LULLABY

Sleep, my little conscience, sleep,
Or silent be if you must weep,
There have been such fearful deeds:
But do not flinch whoever bleeds,
Dig your snout inside your sty,
Snort complaisance, friend, and lie.

Grunt, my little wanton, grunt,
Let the poor ones take the brunt;
Always keep your pockets lined,
And take what profit you may find;
Let others sow that you may reap
And sleep, my little porker, sleep.

Doze, my little treasure, doze,
Anaesthetise your piggy nose;
Let the world go cruelly by,
You're alive who'e'er may die.
Put a penny in the tin
And that will keep you free from sin.

INCIDENT AT CARNAC

Of course you know there's nothing in my mind
Or in my heart inimical to you!
What? Hurt you! No, believe me, love, I find
The whole affair a bind. What could I do?
What say? For any chance to speak at all, some
                                                               luck!
We walked - she talked and talked along the shore -
Dear God! It was a river run amok!
Language made water, thought a Severn bore!
Then I considered murder, looked indeed
For some convenient stone, wondered if
A limpet might give poison or a seaweed
Tetanus - anything, my love - a cliff
To shove her over, quicksand, drown at speed –
Instead, my smile, my upper lip grew stiff.

JANE

Never looking, always peeping,
Mostly grinning, sometimes weeping,
Never walking, always leaping,
Mostly running, sometimes creeping,
Never sowing, always reaping,
Mostly scattering, sometimes heaping,
Never still except when sleeping,
Like a nestling always cheeping,
      Fidget
      Midget!

ON HEARING TIPPET'S FOURTH QUARTET

First thoughts are no
Expectations disarranged
All seems exactly as it should not be
Deliberately opposite
Hard
The outrage is personal
The thrust at first seems outward from the human
Beyond the twitching stars
Beyond time turned inside out
Beyond the mathematic curve
Into that region of unweathered thought
Where, expressed in dance, the first strong steps
In pulsing meditation throb
The radiating centre

But no
A flash of humour
Reorganises rearranged resources
The journey is triumphantly internal
Human after all
Down through the fat and dirt of life
Into that quiet garden of the self

On the first morning
Of the first day
Of the first Spring
In the first Garden
We offer love

A hole in a western bank of cloud
Through which the morning can be seen
Trapped in the evening dark
And though we know that we are happy
We weep because we know

INDIFFERENT LIGHTS

(TWO POEMS FOR TEACHERS)

SCRATCHINGS ON THE GLASS

(1)

When I was young
The cakes my mother made
Were perfect, light and soulless,
Rolling off the production line like machines
Each one reaching the same high level of
                compromised mediocrity,
While the cakes her mother made were alive
Hard in some places
Sometimes lumpy in the middle
Like living bodies with bones and soft glands
And some unmentionable parts which you put
Discreetly on the side of your plate

Now I am old
The cakes I make are like dead animals
Hard and dry and furry with little pieces in them
While the cakes she makes are just like home

As for our daughters
Neither of them bakes at all
And our son cooks and eats nothing but curries

(2)

Said he:
> To me you are perfection

Said she:
> Perhaps I talk too much?

Said he:
> If talking
> Is what perfection is doing today
> Then so be it

(3)

On Friday, the factory where I worked for thirty
> years
Was closed forever;
On Saturday, men came with bulldozers to knock it
> down
And carted it away in lorries;
Now, for the first time, moonlight can shine into my
> bedroom
Through a dark blue wound in the sky;
Why can a man not have both moon and work?

(4)

The household cat sits straight in a bedroom
> window;
His purpose to observe and defend his territory;

Soon he might rise and stretch in his predatory
                                         manner
And think of milk or tinned meat; or on the other
                                         hand
He might sleep now and dine later, or stay where
                                         he is
And rule the world as one who is indispensable.
Beyond the roses, an old civil servant watches
Knowingly, with something approaching
                                         admiration.

(5)

When I sleep with the windows open because of the heat
Street noises, hollow noises seep between the floating
                                         curtains
And bring tremors, restiveness.

What footsteps now below
Strutting on the tight pavement? Whose hard heels caress
                                         the kerb
Striking catpurrs of promise, calling me with the
Rhythmical summons of castanets?

Old buried fantasies
Rear in the hot bed, ramble between the troublesome
                                         sheets
And the hard damp pillow: dark fear and a quick
                                         pounding heart
Bring strange desires alive

Silence - and I must look:
She stands beneath the street lamp opposite, slim
                            and shining
In cheap stretching silk, feet apart, hand on hip, bag
                                        swinging,
Her body all angles.

No sale. Yet still she lingers.
The night grows warmer, sweaty, breathless. She
                            breaks the tension
With a staccato ripple from her right heel as she
                                      swings
Provocatively round.

And then her face. A mask,
Blank, bland, until the light illuminates the soul
                                          beneath,
Street-dirtied, shop-soiled, bruised by grips and
                                          fingerprints,
Defiant in youth

And suddenly so young,
So vulnerable, so much in need of love and caring,
 Lust gives way to pity. But too late! She's gone
                                  and all I hear
Is mocking feet.

(6)

In South America
The peasants of the mountains and the high plains
Chew coca leaves against the numbing cold
Against hunger and boredom,
Futility, frustration, indignity and hopelessness.
It is a gesture of defiance, a grudging acquiescence
And a necessary anaesthetic.
In Britain, the unemployed smoke cigarettes.

(7)

Outside my window lies an urgent world
Of conflicts, competitions, harmonies,
Livings and dyings, failures and successes.
But someone has scratched words upon the glass
And when I try to make sense of them
The view loses precision and is distorted.
Similarly, when I try to see the world as it is,
The scratches blur my understanding

STAINED WINDOWS

(1)

When I was young I sat in class
And learned about the world outside;
I saw through someone else's eyes
What others thought he should provide.
I dutifully took his word
And never thought it was absurd.

And so my mind was slowly filled
With other people's views and thought,
Persuasions, dreams, opinions, facts -
I learned them all as I was taught.
The window which I have is blurred
No wonder now the world's absurd.

(2)

Marvel said music was mosaic
Of the air
And linked two arts by thought. But it will not
Do. The fact that stone and
Notes are anagrams makes it more cerebral
And less like
What it should be; music is structured feeling.

Epigrams, aphorisms, put limits
On life, make
It simpler than it is. They confuse us
Into thinking that all
Answers can be found in rhetoric, that
Problems can
Be solved just by sitting down and talking.

An image nearly out of Yeats might help. Think
                              of a girl
Dancing to herself on a marble floor,
Beautiful, barefoot, clad
In a simple classical robe. I ought
To accept
The whole - but I can only see the girl!

All art tends to that of the singer. He
Is one who
Travels loaded. In the luggage of his
Skill are bricks and mortar,
Maps of dreams, liars, dirt and silk, and, most
Important,
Microscopes, telescopes and coloured slides.

(3)

I took the bricks and placed them on the ground
In the pattern you see here, filled the spaces
With pink concrete - which stopped it looking too
New - and made a place to bask in the sun.
                I thought it was original.

Then I had to provide some shade, so I
Planted trees round it; a buddleia because
My wife likes butterflies, and an apple tree,
And some roses and a few delphiniums.
                That made it unique.

What followed was obvious: a deck chair,
A loungerbed, a stone semi-circular
Bench, and best of all, - le dernier cri -
A big blue umbrella to sit under.
                It was all my own work.

And I was proud. It was a concrete poem.
Until one day I saw my wife sitting
Among the flowers under the umbrella
And I realised I had made a picture.
                Or rather, a copy.

With the sunlight dazzling between the leaves
It was France in eighteen seventy-four
With the flash of Renoir red from the roses
And the bizarre blue of the canopy
                Au bord de la Seine.

(4)

The room is dim and cold. No fire. One flame
Illuminates the desk beside a keyboard;
An empty wine glass on a dirty cloth
And music paper scattered everywhere:
The smell of poverty, tinged with the sweet
Stink of sickness. Is this the love of God?
Outside, the town is snowbound, hostile, still:
No sound is heard but scratchings from a quill.

(5)

I am no scientist
But this I concede
His brain and my brain
Are the same machine
Work in the same way
With the same controls
The self-same methods

He retains his myths
I adhere to mine
And through these means we
Both hope to make a
Small contribution
To our joint culture
In the name of truth.

(6)

Let us imagine the death of a great pianist
And let us go further and imagine his death
In the middle of, shall we say, a Chopin mazurka

Time here is very definite; there is a before and an
                                                      after.
But what happens at that very precise point
Between two chords, the lifting and the laying of a
                                                      finger?

Does everything go? Early memories in an orchard
With tall grasses brushing across his face in the sun
In that happy time before the war before the war:

To say nothing of the expertise, the technical skill
And interpretive power handed down by a man
Who was taught by a man who learned from the
                                                    composer?

Such a great pianist would be always learning, always
                                                 puzzling;
If, at the moment before the moment, his fingers
                                               discovered
Something new about pianism, what would he do with it?

Would it illumine his whole professional musical
                                                life
And explain something he had been pondering for
                                   many years
Or would it just be added to his store and moved
            over to make room for the next item?

To put it another way: was the record wiped clean,
                                   everything gone?
Nothing left? And if so, where did it go? Was it
                                                just
A series of electrical impulses hiding behind words
                              and music?

And when the woman who loved him and the
                      women who lived with him
Found him slumped over the piano. what did they
                                        think?
Did she say, "I have lost my man!"

Did they say, "The world has lost a great musician.
Such music will never be heard again?"
And none of them think where the brain's store
                                        went?

Did they not think that no matter how much you
                                   live in your mind.
In the end, Time will take its revenge?

FOR COLLEEN, ON OUR THIRTY-EIGHTH WEDDING ANNIVERSARY

There was a date
When hand in hand
We'd vault the gate
Which led us to our promised land,
And there in private pleasure roll,
Surrendering each other's soul
Into an all-engrossing whole.

But thirty-eight!
Almost unmanned,
I climb the gate
And hobble to our promised land
And with some effort roll in pleasure
Seeking to regain our treasure -
Ecstasy beyond all measure.

Though bones may creak
When once we start
A heart will speak
Encouragement to loving heart,
And signs of age will disappear
And with them any lingering fear
That loving much has cost us dear.

Then love returns
With youth's excess,
And passion burns
With all its old delightfulness,
So for that moment we are free
From age and time's infirmity,
And you and I are fused in we.

CODA

So will you please, dear loving wife,
Accept this hymn to passionate life,
As ours has been, I trust will be
Continuing perpetually.
And may my epitaph now be
He loved his friend devotedly;
And even to the end of life
Remained a husband to his wife.

IN BARBARA HEPWORTH'S GARDEN - ST IVES

Her accent was pure;
She spoke received English Garden:
There is no originality
As with Monet;
This is no Bodnant,
There are no views of distant hills;
She has not painted with colour
Like Gertrude Jekyll
Nor has Lutyens laid her garden out.
No - it is all quiet;
Domestic.

Much inherited,
Still, it is her disposition,
Her piece of mind made lovely ground,
Hortus conclusus,
Garden inclusive.
Tradition now, the past made quick,
Misty with flowers and pregnant shrubs
And fringed lonely paths;
The work and frame
One consummation
Growing outwards
From her studio.
And here the altars,
Wayside chapels, memento mori
Spiritual milestones, pieces
Of tamed granite

Civilised timber
Deeply imbued with love, permeate
With time, shaped by the spirit
Of ancient places,

Put here for us,
For meditation;
The holiness
Of earth our home..

FROM THE LIBRARY AT THE CENTRE OF THE UNIVERSE

IN THE CHART ROOM

1

All human thought is here, and hope and love.
Plato himself used that desk over there
And on that stool beside it, Socrates
Would perch and close his eyes and question on:
That bay was Aristotle's - not for him
The comfort of a seat, no - he would plod
Round and round, dictating as he went.

II

Old captains hugged the coast: they found their way
By creeping close to rocks and white-washed capes.
At night they anchored under starry skies
And slept round watch fires on a stony beach.
They shipped no pilot nor his tattered chart,
But trusted to their knowledge of the sea
And beat their oars in rhythm with the waves.

III

How many volumes line these miles of shelves,
Stretching, it seems, as far as time will reach,
Each one agleam with self-important print?
And yet they all, each dissertation, tract,
All papers, manifestoes, thoughts, ideas.
All theories and subtle disquisitions
Are notes depending from those greatest three.

IV

No matter what the Pope said, stars obey
Laws of four dimensions, and they turn
In complicated orbits quite unmoved
By orders from a tiny clouded globe:
Their routes projected by a different rule,
Their maps compiled from what is not what ought,
Old sailors trusted to the stars, not faith.

A READING IN THE HISTORY DEPARTMENT
(Three Cracked Trumpet Calls and a Meditation)

1

We have seen a maddened people as they strut along the shore,
In their hearts a fever running, in their minds a glut of gore,
    And the banners they were thrusting
    And the leader they were trusting
Was the old malicious liar who lives and breathes for war!
    Yes, the fancy of the tribe
    Was the old familiar bribe
'I will lead you on to glory if you bow to me in awe'.

Enough! Enough! No more! We have watched it all before!

We have seen them in their triumph when they thought the world was theirs
For their leader, for their nation, for themselves and for their heirs,
    And the innocents they slaughtered
    And the prisoners they tortured
Were their guarantee for ever against vengeance and despair.
    Yes, the delusion of the tribe
    Was the old familiar bribe
That brutality to others will keep them safe from care

Such ideas are not rare: we may find them everywhere.
.

II

Kill truth first; then people. Burn books, shut
                                           mouths,
Spread fear. Alter laws and pervert justice.
Seek out crippled minds and those who harbour
                                           grudges
And give them exercise to glut their spite.
Set up a central agency of terror
And let it ooze by whispers; make the night
Hideous and unhealing with foul acts;
Twist deeds for blackmail, thus to brutalise:
Take power and use it with such cruelty
That you can say, 'Now evil be my good'.

Yes, but to live in such a fearful land
And feel the sides close in! To clog the nose
In scarves and still be choked by acrid smoke
Of hate; to turn the timid eyes aside
Yet not avoid such sights as sear the retina
And stay in place for ever, tinting
What's seen; to hear such lamentations
As would fracture stones in pity; to live
Swathed in a black and insubstantial cloak
Of rumour; to hold out hand and touch death.

Then fear to close the eyes, descend the steps
To that dark cellar where the heart is kept,
Starving to death. Here drift black nightmares
More horrible for being real. Discarded,
Naked corpses, heaped in piles, unburied,
Left to rot beneath the streaming skies;
Around them drag their keepers, pallid ghosts,
Half-dead and sinking. What spirit peeps out
Through windows of their flesh? No sound; none:
Nothing but vacant stare of absency.

And that's your harvest: now is time to pay.
The very things which threw you up will heave
You down - malfeasance, treachery, rage, lust,
Malice, impudence, perjury, envy.
Outside, the world is working for your end
But none more so than you. You cannot talk
And have meaning, nor meet eyes in friendship.
Your people leave and circumvent your orders.
You have lost love and killed life. What's left?
Think on: best kill yourself now. Let's have done.

III

We have seen a beaten people as they straggle in the
                                                                           waste
With their fatherland in ruins and their politics
                                                                          disgraced;
We have seen them beg for comforts from the
                                                             people they'd have killed
As they starve among destruction which they
                                                          themselves have willed –

    Enough! Enough! No more!
    We have heard it all before.

A MINUTE FROM THE HOROLOGICAL INSTITUTE

    Foucault perceived it
    The circular swing
    Saw that it banished
    The eight-legged horse
    And the one-eyed man:

    Thought that it ended
    The self-eating snakes
    The man with the scythe
    Replaced the Age d'Or
    With the Belle Epoch

Misunderstood the
Circularity
Thought it repeated
Eternally; wanted
It all for science:

Did not realise
He had created
Not a cultural
Artefact but an
Inhuman tyrant:

On what would flex and
Breathe, imposed a shape;
Made Time an engine,
Space a diagram,
Man a conqueror.

WHISPERING GALLERY
OR IN THE BELFRY DURING A FULL
PEAL OF BELLS

... it is a truth universally acknowledged poor Tom's a'cold....my brother he is in Elysium they give you chicking in the 'orspital because we was too many beware of Greeks as headstrong as an allegory for God's sake hold your tongue remember my blood, toil and tears in your orisons roll up that brave new world I am therefore I stink

I would the cook was of my mind

Who calls so loud? And is old Double dead?

OLD MEN REVISIT

Old men revisit places where
They spent their youth, a landscape which,
In friendship's terms, excludes despair,
And mollifies their desperate itch.
      In time, I too, must pay my debt.
      Not yet, ah no, not yet!

Old men return to haunt the boy,
To praise his first attempts at song,
And, for an hour or more, enjoy
The luxury of being young.
      In time, I too, must pay my debt.
      Not yet. ah no, not yet!

A row of trees which lines a dream,
A fussy ferry, brown-choked foam,
The scream of seagulls, clouds of steam,
This is the countryside of home.
      In time, I too, must pay my debt.
      Not yet, ah no, not yet!

For I have mountains still to friend,
Hard roads to follow, all uncharted,
Before I take that final bend
And homeward come to where I started.
      In time, I too, must pay my debt.
      Not yet, ah no, not yet.

A SHROPSHIRE ROAD

Behind me lies the bright side,
Is the warm side, lies the home side,
Is the light side, is the right side,
    As I go down the hill.

Before me lies the gloom side,
Is the cold side, lies the old side,
Is the doom side, is the tomb side
    As I go down the hill.

Let no one try to hold me
As I plunge down the track,
To catch me nor enfold me
Nor wish to hold me back -

For where I walk will you walk,
To where the world is still,
Yes, my pace will be your pace
To the bottom of the hill.

TROPHY WIVES

Once they have died and, safely, can't reply,
Old widows spin fine yarns about their men,
Webs of conceit they use to justify
Their low position in that regimen
Where once they served. It is not quite a lie,
More different lighting, so alternate heights
Are emphasised, to show how very high
They were, and how they understood their rights
And how they always were too brave to cry;
How they knew best - to put it without gloss -
And did his job, and theirs, without a sigh,
And yet, in every case, gave him the kudos.
Old spiders kill their mates and suck them harder
And hang them, like a trophy, in their larder.

SONNETS OF PAIN

(1)

No! I don't care! That's how I feel today!
Tomorrow may be acid in my mind
As yesterday was bile. Oh, let him play
His game of spite, just now I'm disinclined
To exercise myself at his expense:
No, I'll not weep nor grind my teeth nor mope -
I've dug my mound and round it built my fence,
And I will live inside it without hope.
Oh, I have dreamed the past into new shapes,
Repainted images and scrubbed the past,
Wandered through gorgeous corridors and spent
Hours in sunny uplands, enjoyed escapes
With him, - then found when woken all too fast
Achilles still is sleeping in his tent.

(2)

A pale watery gleam glows through the mist. Some
Hope from that. Perhaps the ice will soften, melt
At last. The coldest minutes cannot numb
Like such an ice wave, personally dealt.
Wet ice is not so cruel as deep snow;
Cold skies are not so gloomy as thick cloud;
Unhappy feelings not so hard as woe;
A neutral spirit's better than one cowed!
This thaw might fortify my former friend,
Perhaps it's not a matter of decree,
Who knows - it might not be at any price?
The season's shift might give a warmer end
To all my chilled desires. And now, oh, see!
A wintry sun is lighting up the ice!

(3)

No post again today and none I guess
Tomorrow; no footsteps at the door, no
Cheery rattle from the box. Is my address
Not known? Or scribbled out? Forgotten? No!
That cannot be the case! It's spite or hate,
Or planned indifference, not pity, no!
It's not the twistings of a passive fate,
Nor love's blank, other face; no, never! No!
How can I grieve with nothing in my hand?
No brief initials, no calm regrets, no
Signs of cold discourtesy, no bland
Conceding of my unimportance, no
Paper which was once warmed by his hand –
No post again today and none, I know.

(4)

Yes, I'm an academic; I love books:
I love their smell, the whiteness of their pages;
I love their permanence, their ancient looks,
The power of their texts and all which that presages;
 Such wisdom lined my shelves when you were
                                                                young,
It was my pleasure then to let you read it
And you responded to their siren song
By taking knowledge when you seemed to need it.
Yet now that unanimity is gone,
Two minds in patient study have been parted,
You your way, leaving me to work alone
With still some hope, although now weary-hearted.
As books are dead without an eye to scan them,
So fires are out without a breeze to fan them.

(5)

With what steep steps we lurch along the way,
 Each step the tougher as the load grows more
And heavier yet as each heart has its say
And pushes on to make itself more sore.
And yet we'd not be free - for that's our bug -
We lug our pain, enjoy the greater weight,
Talk with frail smiles of how we love to hug
Our dearest agony of wish and hate.
Yet, strangely, as we bend and shuffle on,
Each pace removes us further from the cause,
And what was unendurable is none
So heavy when we stand and stretch and pause.
Our load slips from us with no parting pain
As we walk on and leave it in the lane.

(6)

Yet when it came, it came with ease. No show
Of pomp, no snarling trumpet, no great drum;
The day was simple, dawn a common glow -
Nothing pretentious told us what had come.
Did Eden start like this? No creaking gate,
No laser searchlights, no compulsive green,
No here is Adam, here is Eve, his mate,
No hint of triumph in the quiet scene?
It must have been, for so it was ordained
And so were we the playthings of some shot
Or, more than that, we were the ones who gained
Our meeting through some deeply thought-out plot.
So here we stand, amazed at what has been,
For ours was the light on the answer machine.

(7)

No plastic smiles, no cheerful smiling face,
No absolute pretence; let all things be
As they must be; take heart and do not chase
The necessary clouds that we may see
An artificial sun. Oh, do not, please
Obscure yourself behind a false good health!
Smile when your spirit laughs and do not tease
Us with a show of mock, pretentious wealth.
We know, you see, what ills afflict you now;
We know what hurts you casually have taken;
We've heard your voice and heard the pain's hard
                                                              crow
And guessed the fears that your troubles waken.
If you can bear your torments, tell it true,
So we may share your sad condition, too.

HOMING

In the classroom they are planning a painting
Young children together, planning a picture
Sir Francis Drake
Returning from his journey round the world
And being welcomed by his Sovereign

And eighty miles away
At the bottom of a ward
A woman is coming to her journey's end:
She lies in a nest of pillows
Curled up, shrinking,
While round her floats a pattern of nurses
Professionally cool in the sight of death

  There will be others present too, in their picture
  Lords and excited Ladies
  And things like ships and houses
  And possibly some country folk.
  This week's task is to draw the main characters
  Next week, or even later
  They will fill in the background
  Add the trees and water
  Work out the perspectives
  Relationships
  And add lots and lots of colour

And eighty miles away.
In Liverpool
This week's task is to draw the curtains

For all of you
On your setting forth
And your home-coming
Let it be so
With no pain
But that which is appropriate

WALKING HOME

The music pumping through my head
As I walked home by Brincliffe Edge
With something of a spring in my step
And a simple thankfulness in my heart
Because you had come through
The music I was walking to
Faded and cleared
As though a curtain was drawn across it
When the moon slid
A magnificent full-bodied stripper
White and round
As though throwing off the rags of cloud
And stood there
Naked
Odalisque

The male with silence in his head
Stood in silence
And stared at the white female in the sky
In her simplicity and silence
Ignoring him
Almost a deliberate confrontation of
                                  opposites

How long I stood
I do not know by real time
Head time, moon time
An eternity, a thought for ever
Until my masculinity
Revolting at the spell
Threw a male critical thought
Into my consciousness
I thought that now you are free of her
That moon
You have been cut free
And more than that
You have become the moon

The music rose again
Not triumphant in quite the same way
As I walked on
Thinking that we had defeated her at last
And would not change in her way
And I could not resist
Shooting cheeky glances up at her
As I thought we did not need her any more

And she, of course,
Quite properly went on ignoring me

THIRTY NINTH WEDDING ANNIVERSARY

No, Thirty-Nine is not a proper number;
It's more a bridge, a sort of anything which spans;
A nothing, no! I'm sure it has its fans
But, as for me, it's classed as attic lumber
With other junk, like Six or Twenty-Two,
Like Nine or Twenty; even Thirty-Three
Has nothing much to say to you and me;
For proper numbers carry sense; they do
What is expected of them; they're the key
To all the ages. Could Twenty-One fall down?
Or Diamond Sixty fail? Oh no, they're free;
Like Golden Fifty they will take the crown!
And yet, poor Thirty-Nine has lots to share
For, through his agency, we're still a pair.

THE LEGEND OF SPAD

A Year In the Life of an Ordinary Dunnock

1

The Folk of the Field

That year, warm rain was early; low grey clouds
Came swelling from the west, driven by winds
Perfumed with fantasies of southern lands,
Which made the heart beat faster. And, after
Solid rain, came sun and showers, frost, dews,
Hail and thunder, snow and mists and tempests -
Winter and summer mixed - the sort of thing
Which makes us such a hardy, island race.

  Then Spring came dancing through the lonely field
  And trailed green fingers gently through the grass,
  Touched all the tips of branches with new life
  Along the hedge and on the standing trees.
  Buds burst and, on a morning when the sun
  Grew hot, sprang flowers spinning from the earth
  In yellow, white and purple, face upwards
  To be kissed. And in the hedge, in burrows,
  In trees, hollows in the ground, in anywhere
  That parents found of use, came bold, demanding,
  Vulnerable infants, wide-eyed, greedy;
  And hens and cocks went scurrying through the world
  On hectic business.
                      Deep underground,

The badger stretched and yawned and drew his
                                          bedding
Upward to the sun; the mole worked harder,
Scrabbling through the roots, clearing his roads
In frantic lust for worms; the hedgehog trotted
Through the heavy grass and quite ignored
The hare basking in the shadows of the hedge.
For all was harmony, endeavour, work,
Amongst the varied folk, until the field
Was dizzy with the sights and sounds of life.

Along the hedge, just where an ancient thorn,
Now young in white, gave way to elder trees,
Among the linnets, wrens and chaffinches,
Upon a branch quite near a main road through,
Lived Spad, a dunnock, and his lovely wife.
Now he was in his prime, being one year old,
And full of love and power and impudence,
And all was put at service of his mate.
For she was, so he thought, so truly beautiful
That he could scarcely bear to leave her side.
He called her Spadgette; she was his first wife
And would become the pattern for the rest.
But now she was the object of his life,
And where she went, went he, attentive, watchful,
And when she hopped, he hopped alongside too.
She had the slenderest beak of all her kind
And brightest, roundest eyes. She was housewifely
In her dress, neat and clean, but not too smart
And yet not drab, demure in grey and brown,
And always glossy, speckless, delicate.

To see her spear an insect with her beak
As they went hunting through the shorter grass
Filled Spad's young heart with joy; and when she
                                        hopped,
The supple movement of her wings and thighs
Would make him close his eyes and curl his toes
Around a twig for very ecstasy.
But when she looked at him and dropped her head
In that particular way and spread her wings
And lifted up her tall, why then his heart
Melted within his breast! For she was love
And she was his and he could see no further.
And yet, for all her quiet ways, she worked
Him hard, because she knew it takes much drive
To make an egg, and in her patient
And persistent calls on his young strength
 She bound him closer to her, until he
Could not sleep against her side without deep
Dreams of love and wake to find them real.
So hard they worked at coming parenthood
And Spad was equal, just, to her requests
That even all the wrens were much impressed.

 But oh! how different when the eggs came through!
 Told to mind his feet; told to keep quiet;
 No room to rest his head; hushed if he closed
 His eyes in case he snored and, like as not,
 Ejected briskly from his nest to sulk upon a twig
 Or hunt for bugs alone among the weeds.
 His feathers ragged and uncombed, his eyes
 Lacklustre and betrayed, he drifted like
 A shadow through the darkness of the hedge

And knew himself bereft,
When sorrow gripped his heart and squeezed his
                                  love,
'Til he could scarcely peck or cheep or hop,
He thought of Life and what it meant to him
And what his purpose was - and felt belittled.

Yet that was heavenly bliss compared to when
The chicks were hatched! After the shock of seeing
Such draggled things, naked and damp, panting,
Pink and black, and, worse! the look of doting
Deep in Spadgette's eyes, rose deep and freezing
Waves of outrage. To call those his! To think
That he must sweat and strain from dawn to dusk,
To fly and hover, hunt, pounce, and gather;
Fight with another husband for the sweetest seed
Or plumpest grub; regard the setting sun
And plan another trip running into dark,
Knowing he would be up before the light!
And all for things with beady, loveless eyes;
All yellow gape and stomach! Then to clean
The mess they made! Hard payment for a little
Pleasure - always hungry. always tired.
Ever reluctant.

                Yet he did it! Yes,
He flew his trips, competed for the best,
And hated every minute of his life;
And in the twilight, when the nest was quiet,
Would stir upon his branch, too tired for sleep,
And give a little cheep for manhood's sake,
And wonder on his destiny. For he

Had yearnings far outside his nest, beyond
The hedge and field; desires and hopes and fears
Which stirred his heart and brought a gleam
To a tired eye. There must be more than this,
He thought before he slept, more for a Spad
To do than fetch and carry for a brood of chicks.

II

A Judgement and an Execution

So Spad sat glooming, crouched upon a branch
Between two thorns, in the very self-same place
His granddad mooned some several summers past.
As yet the sky was dark and all the hedge
Was quiet. His brood and Spadgette slept, tucked
All together in a rush of feathers.

Despite fatigue he was awake. His wings
Ached and his throat was dry; his eyes
Were sore; his beak was tender with the taps
And pokes of hungry young. His thirst was great
And yet he would not move; the night was full
Of dangers and he must not leave the nest.

Time passed. He kept his restless watch. The world
Turned grey and cool. He ruffled his feathers
And fluffed them out. Something shrieked in the
                                        wood
Behind him and he thought of foxes.

                              At last
A pallid gleam lit up the eastern sky,
With silver first, then strengthened into gold
And finally deep red, shading into pink.
Spad shivered in his hedge and gazed across
The field, looking for signs of life.
And, as he stared, a thick white mist which lay
Upon the grass was touched with rising warmth
And writhed and twisted as it melted.

                              Spad
Stretched. Soon he would fly for food. But even
As he yawned and shook himself, his eyes blinked
Open in astonishment, his beak gaped
Wide, his morning whistle died intestate.
Fear slowly froze his muscles until movement
Was impossible and breathing painful.
For there, not twenty yards from where he sat,
Manifest in the parting of the mist,
Silent as statues, resolute as rocks,
Black in that bright morning, a ring of birds
Was sitting on the ground, as full of menace
As the shadow of a noose.
                        What it meant
Young Spad could not yet tell, but he knew enough
To keep his beak shut and his feet quite still,
And hoped that Spadgette and their young would
                                        sleep
Or wake silently.

             A sudden movement.

The ring was broken and he saw inside
To where a solitary wretch was squatting,
The prisoner, alone before his judges.
There was, or had been, some brief colloquy -
Spad was too far away to hear them speak -
But now, it seemed, the crisis had been reached.
Two birds swaggered up and took their place
On either side the miscreant.
       The sun
Rose higher, waxed stronger. Shadows blackened,
Shortened. Spad could not blink.
         There came no sign,
But suddenly the bully boys rose up
And fell like leaping panthers, landing
On the bird beneath, wings arched, heads low, beaks
              curved
Time and again they struck, working together
In fearful sympathy, while the members
Of the court watched motionless, like gargoyles
On a roof.
     When all was done and they stood
Casually by the poor thing on the ground
They wiped their beaks on clumps of grass, and
              preened
Their feathers, twisting round to reach the wings
With delicate, fastidious nibbling
Movements. When they were satisfied that not
A trace of any evidence remained,
They strutted back to join the ring, their duty
    done.

Then, with a rush of wings, the squadron
Rose and twisted, flirting with its shadow
On the ground, formed and reformed over the field
And flew heavily away.

Spad waited and watched.

After a while he cocked his head and squinted
At the sky to see if all was safe. Then,
Sleek and knowing, yet wary all the same,
He flew to where the corpse lay sweating in
The sun. He had no pity and very
Little fear. But curiosity could
Occupy his mind. And so he pondered
The deep gashes in the neck, the sightless eyes,
All stained with blood. And wondered what great
                              power
Could make him offer up his throat without
A fight? What discipline, what laws, could bind
                              so fast?
Head on one side, Spad hopped around,
And peered and jumped and leapt across the feet
And paused to contemplate the savage beak.
But there was nothing that dead thing could say
In explanation of its brutal end.

Already mites were climbing from the grass
And beetles mustering at the prospect

Of a feast. Spad pecked them off, but even
This good food did nothing to allay
The dark around his heart. There was danger
Here, he thought, for him and all his kind.

Then Spadgette chirrupped to him from the nest
And called him to his work. And so that day
Was spent like all the rest in labouring.
Yet even so, while he was harrying
The insect world, his mind was drawn
Inevitably back to that dead bird and all
The grimmest fears of what it might portend.

III

A Pastoral Interlude

The summer ripened and the nestlings grew.
The field was full of seed, the hedge of grubs,
Enough and more for all. For one short week
Spad and his wife led all their thriving brood
Along the hedgerow while they learned to feed.

When Spad compared his bright-eyed, sturdy
                                          young.
And saw how each could now fend for itself,
With what his cousins reared, a single lump,
Lazy and demanding, fat and growing
Bigger, still requiring food thrust down its

Throat, he felt a kind of pride in being
                              Father.
  Spadgette herself was all concern,
  All fuss, and stalked the little ones for signs
  Of hunger, when she would peck the ground
  To demonstrate the necessary actions.
  Spad would merely watch and call out orders
  Which no one heeded, but as a mere male
  He was content to be allowed his say.

His purpose was to watch for predators;
  But who would harm a family of dunnocks?
  The vixen and her cubs were far away,
  Driven by hounds to seek another den;
  Shrews were abundant in the hedgerow runs
And easy for the kestrel and the owls;
Even the rabbits had bred their way to numbers
After the great disease and made good prey
For any stoats with families to feed.
No, all seemed safe and quiet enough, except
There was a seagull squawking overhead,
A harsh and frightening. greedy, alien cry,
Which made Spad nervous. He had seen it steal
An egg and stand in full view of the nest
With yolk sliding from the angle of its beak
And tread upon the shell and walk away.
Nothing seemed safe from this rapacious bird,
Provided it was stolen rapidly.
There was a time when Spad and all the birds
Who lived with him would rise like a dense swarm
Of insects to mob him off. But as he

Wheeled above, Spad sensed he was replete.

                              Yet
When he slid away down some long valley
Of the air. Spad breathed more easily, and
Followed in the wing beats of a pigeon
To where it fanned the seed and so obtained
A second and third breakfast free of charge.

Ah, happy days! Ah, golden days! Such times
Of hot sun and the snuff of rich warm dust,
Of fruitful fields, of innocence and work,
Of family feeling dimly understood -
The treasures of the mind in retrospect.
Spad took reward and stood in grace, himself
                                          fulfilled.
And then one day his dream was done!
Without a backward glance his chicks had flown;
No thanks, no time to say goodbye; a flutter
Of the wings against a gentle breeze;
The springing of a twig against the nest,
And all had gone! Not one remained to comfort
Or cajole. A mud-lined bowl of sticks was
What he had to show for all his work.
                                    Then
Spadgette said, "The summer, dear, is not so
Far advanced. We have our nest complete.
Let's do it all again!"
                          Her eye was liquid,
Full and gleaming, her plumage glossy
And her tones persuasive. She looked at him

And Spad was young again, for he was mortal.
He leapt to her and she was loving back.

Though when he rested, cheeping very low,
He wondered whether he had been too rash
And whether what he'd done would bring regrets

IV

The Death of Owl

A rumour ran along the hedges, passed
Among the thorns and leaves, slid across
The branches, paused in the weeds, stirred the
                                                  grass
In a small tempest, gathered force and sped
From short thick beak to needle beak, from seed
Crusher to grub spearer. And youngsters felt
Their parents' quick dismay as gossip turned
To fact: old Owl was dying!
                                Oh misery
And fear and sweet relief that such a proud
And strict authoritarian should
Be stretching to his final, gasping breath!
For Owl had ruled the folk along the field
With a stern gaze which quite unnerved them all.
It seemed that he could penetrate their minds
And hear their thoughts, and that same stare
Could make their muscles tense so that they were

Bereft of any movement and, paralysed,
Stood still at his command.

                        He ruled them well,
With wisdom and with justice. Quick mercy
He knew not. His wisdom came from memory;
His justice from his genes - for justice is
The only kindness which cannot corrupt.

And then the summons came: all nest-holders
Must gather underneath the old oak tree
Which dominates the coppice by the stream.
So forth the people streamed, all difference
Forgotten in the crush. Hawk sprinted
Side by side with wren; kestrel politely
Let the finch go first. They hopped from branches,
Fluttered from the trees, ran through the grasses,
Swam slowly up the stream, until the crowd,
Positioned on the ground some twenty feet
Beneath a leafless branch - a spot where grass
Was sparse - were silent, scarcely daring
To draw breath.

All eyes were raised to that articulate
And sombre form so heavily above them.

The neck untwisted and the face appeared;
And then those huge, engrossing, pallid eyes
Reduced their heart beats to a timid tapping.

And so they held, watcher and watched combined,
As they had done so many times before.
But then, it seemed, the eyes were slowly dimmed;
The power failed; the discs were filled with tears
And Owl was seen as lonely, frightened, old.
A sigh disturbed the watchers on the ground
Like a wind that riffles gently through the wheat.
Owl shook his head to clear his sight and brain
And thus addressed them - or rather, this is
What he would have said had he the power
To speak in words. But, through the agency
Of feather, beak and claw, communication
Was established there.
              "Oh, my dear people,
I have not called you here to say good bye,
Although goodbye is what I have to say. No!
We have been a people good enough,
Living in various harmonies.
I have been proud to oversee you all,
And there have been times when 1 have saved you
From creatures who would smash our way of life.

But that was in my prime, when I could see,
When I could sweep on muffled wings above
The bending grass, pounce like a cat and tear
Like an eagle. But now, too many times
I miss my prey, and at this time, just now,
When even my great strength would have been
                                taxed,
There comes to us a threat I cannot meet,
For I am feeble. faltering and weak."

The folk were silent as a steady cloud
Which threatens storms and yet will not deliver.

"Oh, my dear friends! For how I love you all!
I dreamt last night of such catastrophe
That will fall on you from the skies, destroy
You all, elders and nestlings all, a foe
So organised, so numerous and strong
That you will all be killed without a chance!"

At this a coletit fainted, so fervent
Were the thoughts, so tense the atmosphere.
And even Seagull, prowling round the edge,
Was silent, head cocked sideways in the sun.

"The thought quite weakens me. 1 can no more.
I feel my life is ending now!"
          At this
His talons loosened on the branch, his eyes swept up
And suddenly he fell, a lifeless body
On the earth.
     There was no move, though every eye
Perceived the falling corpse. Owl lay grotesquely
On his back, one leg stretched to the perch above,
The other by the scrape it made on landing.
His beak was driven deep into the litter,
His eyes were shuttered tight against the light
For ever.
      There was no cry or wailing.
Each bird was solemn yet consolable.

Then one by one, in order of their place,
They rose and left, hopping or fluttering
As their temperament declared was apt.
Some few went to the corpse - Spad among them -
For a moment's thought or brooding, before
Leaving for their various domains.

When Spad returned, he found the eggs were laid,
And Spadgette, flushed and happy, slimmer too.
Was proudly sitting in the brimming nest.

That night the moon was full, an owling night,
And as Spad looked across the skies,
Beyond the nearer glory of the heavens,
A tiny star fell in a burst of light,
As though some journey's end had just been
                                        reached.
Its fire was kindled in an answering gleam
Deep in Spad's solemn, watching, anxious eye.

V

The Black Plague

No rain had fallen now for many weeks:
The grass was parched and white; the leaves were
                                        thick
Like blackening tongues. The earth was either
                                        hard,
Like brick, or friable, like dust, and when

A hot wind blew, then little twisters curled
Across the field and into everything,
Until the hedge was white with summer frost.
Evenings were heavy, ominous and dark;
Rumbles of trouble came like thundering
In far hills. At night, the hedgefolk cowered
As lightning flickered intermittently
On the fringes of the world. They sat in
Torpid silence and imagined who knows
What great nightmares.
                        Spadgette, who turned
Her eggs and settled down again, spread wide
Her wings and fluffed her feathers out, as though
She would keep house even on judgement day.
Spad pondered on it all and watched her brood.

And then one day the promised torment came:
The sky was overcast, the sun was red
But hot, when surging from the south came skeins
Of birds, trailing side by side, more and more
Until the light was all but blotted out;
Like a huge twisting, panting organism,
Shrieking and twittering, bellying low
Above the field. The many thousands paused
But for a moment, wheeling before they dropped
Like paratroopers landing at the ready.
It seemed there was a blizzard of the birds,
Nor that there could be air for such a crowd.
And soon the field was heaving with them all
Like an old man's blanket under lice.
And each of them was pecking vigorously,

Voraciously devouring everything.

At the first onset, those who could, escaped,
Spad with them, rising from the hedge like dust
From a beaten mat, and fled in terror.
All day he shivered, hiding in a ditch,
Among the litter, underneath a dock,
Behind a moving clump of stinging nettles.
And even here he did not feel secure,
Although his eyes were tightly closed, his beak
Low to the ground. A craven dunnock,
Frightened for his life and quivering with guilt!
And so he was and so he stayed, inert.
For he could hear the din of greedy birds,
Feel through his claws their trample on his field,
Dread in his heart their impact on his life,
Fear for his future under such a dark
And powerful, cruel dispensation.

In time the sky grew darker. Spad shifted
Low among the leaves, startled a scurrying
Shrew, which vanished down an avenue
Of docks. He calmed his thumping heart.
         The sun
Set among a glow of gold and purple clouds.
Spad crawled up into the long grasses.
Once there, he saw the hordes depart. They rose
Like locusts in a swarm, black bits against
The light, swirling in their multitudes. Yet
Awful though this was, it was the sound
Which made him flinch, a din which passed
           beyond
Mere noise into the realms of violence and pain.

And when it drawled away to nothing, ceasing
Below a whisper, he stayed unmoving,
Stunned and empty headed.
                          Then came hunger,
Stirring, driving him to action. And with
Action came remembrance. He must forage
For himself and for his wife. His wings stretched
And eagerly he set course for his nest.

Above his field he banked, intending to swoop
 For food. But then he stalled and twittered round
When he perceived the damage to the earth,
Where all was scarred and scratched, tined and torn.
So many claws, so many hungry beaks,
So many squabbles savagely pursued;
So little space to hold so many birds;
So little food to share among the hordes,
Had left his garden pitifully wronged,
Its pride betrayed, its purpose overcome,
All order lost, all harmony destroyed:
It lay below him like a battlefield.

Yet worse than what he saw was what he heard!
A wailing rose, a loud lamenting cry,
Throbbing along the margins of the field,
Which struck his heart with fear.
                                 And so with haste,
All thought of self forgotten, he turned and
                                              dived,
Seeking his nest and mate. But what a sight
Invaded now his eyes as anxiously
He flew along the hedge! It seemed each branch

Was stripped, a skeleton, bared of all fruit,
Each nut cracked and eaten; some twigs shattered
By the weight of many thieves, hung shredded,
White, torn. Down every way he looked, he saw
Destruction. And worse; death.
                              Each neighbour's nest
Had been reduced: the branches, feathers, down,
Ruthlessly distributed; the egg shells
Cracked, some hanging crazed in forks, the
                                         contents
Leaking; others starring softly on the ground.
He passed the seagull with its broken neck,
Its yellow beak agape, stuffed with earth.

Home he sped, twisting and turning down each
Thoroughfare, dreading to go, but travelling
Faster yet! And when he came, what sadness
Did he find! His home had not been safe against
Attack. Spadgette lay spread across the ruins
Of the nest, her wings outspread protectively,
Slaughtered in the strength of her maternity.
Her gentle throat was trenched with many gashes;
Her lovely feathers darker, stained with blood;
Her eyes, whose glow could fill Spad's heart with
                                           joy,
Were dulled in looking upward, for mercy
Or deliverance, who can say? Around
Her corpse, her eggs lay shattered, and with them
Lay Spad's hopes.

        He left the place to foxes
And to crows, and flew into the darkness
Of the night. He found a perch and sat there
On his own, wrapped in his wings and, lonely,
Began to whimper, weeping through the night.

VI

The Plague Continues

Next day they came again. This time, it seemed,
In even greater swarms. The risen sun
Had scarcely lit the morning sky before
Their dark wings cast great shadows on the land.
And when they took the field, with what disdain
They gloried in their conquest, posturing
In their sleek uniforms, waddling, bowing,
Paddling in the shallows of their triumph!

What torments were endured by those who owned
The place! Hungry, they saw their food devoured
Before their eyes. Thirsty, they saw their drinking
Water fouled. And still they feared to stir abroad
In case these buccaneers seized their necks
And shook them into death. And so they lurked,
Inexorably weakening in strength,
While over everything they loved was cast
The fluent stink of dehydrating ordure.

And so was Spad, like them, a prisoner.

In happier times, when food was plentiful,
He liked to wander in and out the hedge,
Beneath the leaves and through the strong tall
grass
Or under bushes where the green was thick,
For here he found his richest pickings: beetles,
Spiders, caterpillars, grubs - anything
Which moved in dank rich secrecy. And so
He made a living for himself and family
And left room for others.
                        And now - nothing!
The cupboards of his larder had been swept;
The shelves left bare. In two days all he ate
Was one sick ant that lacked its two back legs,
Hardly a meal to satisfy a hungry
Hedge Accentor!

                        So as the sun moved on,
And heat grew hotter, and his desperate
Situation grew more grim, gradually
He wound his mind up tighter to a tough
Determination to escape. Better
To die from one swift blow than ebb in slow
And painful hunger.
                        The plan was simple:
 It was his hope to reach a stand of trees,
 A place where rooks and jackdaws lived and bred
 Where he might feel secure. And he would wait
 Until the dusk, when all the starling mob
 Had vanished.

			But so great was his hunger,
  And such his vanity, challenged by guilt
  And anger as it was, he would not stay.
   For he must feed before night fell or starve,
  And anyway he could outwit with ease
  A snowfall of marauding predators.

He could get partly there along the hedge
And so he did. working his way not inches
From some raiders in the field. Several times
He thought he must be seen, so slowed his pace
And crept, a darker shadow in the shades.

But came the time when he must make his bid,
Come into the open, take the fearful risk.
Or skulk in hunger, desperately sad.
He shuffled underneath a giant dock
And peered out at the pasture he must
Cross. He could not see his sanctuary:
What filled his vision were the bobbing heads,
The walking beaks, the clawlike hovering wings,
A flash of green and purple from a back,
Incessant movement, fighting, bickering,
As they kicked the world so carelessly about.

Four thousand dunnock heartbeats now to cross!
He took one breath and leapt, aiming for the space
Above the bucking feeders and beneath
The circling, waiting watchers overhead.
For a pause, a strain of twenty wingbeats,
He succeeded, flying straight, flying fast,

Before a screech went up. He saw the open
Beak from which it came and the wild eyes
Rolling up. Like a tidal wave it swept
Across the field, heads lifting, eyes glaring,
Throats squawking, until it seemed he was
The object of all scrutiny and growing hatred.
Soon now he would be marked, chased,
Caught, savaged, plucked surely out of the air,
Torn to a whirl of feathers and allowed
To drop, a lifeless lump.
      Now they were rising,
Narrow wings flapping fast, coming for him,
Driving up to climb above his flight path,
And then to swoop with open claws.
        But already
Those above had seen his tiny frame dart
Over the field and were swerving to start
Their swooping descent.
      Trapped! What could he do?

He worked for greater speed, head down, eyes
         staring.
But it was no good; he was not built for pace.
It could not be long before he would be crushed
Between the upper and lower jaws.

Yet he could dodge! He slipped aside in time
For those attacking from above to miss
Their strike, and then ascended to the space
They left, thereby hoping to leave both parties
Hopelessly entangled.

                    And so he did.
And so it worked and so he gained some space
In which to run.

            Thwarted, they screamed, reformed,
And mobbed again. So many came he must,
This time, be lost. He thought to dive and hoped
This way to break right through their swarms and flee
Hugging the ground, jinking at will, until
He reached his haven.
                        But small chance of that.
The cruel beaks now rising fast towards him
Were gathered tight together, like a band
Of spears in the hands of desperate
And professional homicides.
                            Spad plunged
Straight towards his vicious adversary.
He sought a tiny chink through which he might
Slide unscathed. But none appeared. He could see
The venom in their eyes, hear their shouts grow
                                louder,
They thought they had him dead!
                    But as he dived,
He heard a creaking noise and felt a wind
Was pulling on his tall. And both increased,
Deafening him. The wind grew stronger yet,
Tugging at him, holding him back. The noise
Was hurting deep inside his brain.
                            Just when
It seemed he was to be impaled, a force
Twitched him away, picked him up, sucked him up,

Away, high to safety. Like some small insect
In a thermal draught, he tumbled upwards
Into level air.
                He watched the starlings
Dwindle down below; their shouts receded.
Soon he could scarcely see or hear their fury.

He thought at first that he had died and risen
To that great nest beyond the clouds, where all
The dead make one huge family - until he
Heard the noise and found that he was flying
Without effort, gliding in the slip-stream
Of a huge swan. And all around him
Was the skein, flying steadily, strongly,
With slow, powerful wingbeats. Spad floated
On the waves they made, lucky to be alive.
The swans ignored him; they were about some
Business of their own, which no stray dunnock
Could deflect them from.
                And Spad was happy
Thus to cadge a lift - until he looked below!
He had never been so high in all his life
And the sight of tiny fields and little trees
Terrified and drove him close to panic.
He had no head for heights, and vertigo
Soon had his vision swimming. And oh! besides
It was so very cold! His muscles chilled
And stiffened in the thin air. And so he
Lost control of both his mind and body.
He drifted sideways in the eddying air,

Fell from the currents, spinning sideways down,
And, like a falling leaf, rocked gently
In his progress to the ground.
                                        No one marked
His fall – like Icarus, he came without
A splash and landed in a tuft of trees
Not fifty feet from where he'd planned to be.
Here he was safe and warm and quite unharmed.
Nor did he hear the racket of the swans
As they swept on their way remorselessly.

(VII)

And Ends

That night he slept in better heart, replete
With food and drink, than he had done since first
The starlings came. And in the golden dawn,
When the first rays melted all the wisps of cloud,
He stood upon a low branch in a hedge
And piped a little hymn of thankfulness.
He didn't worry that the land was parched,
The air was dry, the standing wheat was bleached -
The day's heat brought the insect world to life;
His breakfast soon was buzzing round his head
And he had need of it, for he had much
To put back to regain his former strength.

Now where he was, was peaceful, calm and warm
And fairly soon young Spad was feeling bored;
His eyes were bright, his feathers trim and clean,

His opinion of himself was very high,
His stomach was crammed full with insect protein;
But he was in a place he did not know.
And this had two results: the first was that
Because the field was strange, he had no deep
Responsibility towards its welfare,
Which gave him, for the first time in his life
A sort of freedom; he could do just what
He wanted without guilt. The second was, his
Curiosity was roused. Exploring
Was a possibility not limited
By territorial imperatives.

So off he hopped, quite happy for a while
To wander through the hedgerows, free from care
And idly hunting. As he went he whistled
Very soft, the high-pitched squeak of dunnocks
On the prowl.
     The hedge was not much
Different from his own: he scrambled under
        branches,
Hopped over roots, squeezed under weeds and
        took
No notice where he stepped.
       There came a point
He perched upon a twig to take a rest
And look about. He kept very still:
A grasshopper which leapt too near his perch
Was caught and swallowed in one lightning move.
He cleaned his beak beneath his off-side wing
With conscious knowledge of his expertise.

The sun was filtering through the ripening leaves;
A little breeze was stirring them about
And making all the shadows jump across
The dazzling shafts of sun. But Spad could see
Despite the blinding contrast. He studied
The slow movement of a grass snake with great
Care and hopped up to a higher, thinner branch,
In case he was mistaken. Here he was
Confronted by a finch which stared him down
And off. The thump of rabbits attracted
His gaze next and, after that, a squabble
Between two shrews.
      Yet all was quite half-hearted:
It was the drowsy, lazy time of day,
Deep afternoon, when everyone was full
And loth to move. Except Spad, who, because
He was a stranger in the place, had no
Rights save those of passage. And so he sauntered,
Lingered, strolled, but kept on moving
          The hedge
Was running straight towards the little patch
Of woodland, just beyond a tiny, dried-up
River bed. Here, like a stone upon a stone,
Half-shaded, half in light, an old toad sat,
His cat eyes veiled, angling for flies. Spad saw
His liquid tongue spit and take a dozing
Moth right under his nose. And while the old
Lips chumbled on the prey, helped by a wrinkled
Thumb, the eyes opened momentarily.
In their coldness, Spad thought he saw old Owl
And fluttered up to safety in the trees.

As he swung upon a branch, he looked back,
But toad was still, a menace in the heat.
High above, two magpies chattered as they stalked
The canopy, seeking anything
Worth stealing. In a sudden explosion
A pigeon burst away in a falling
Trail of damaged leaves. Soon it was
Blowing resentment from the far side of the wood.
The heat became almost too great to bear:
Shafts of sun, like lances, pierced the grove
And roasted litter underneath the trees:
Flowers wilted in the furious rays.
The magpies flew, their long tails angled down,
Across the fields in some sly cause.

Spad climbed higher, hopping from branch to
                                          branch,
Drawn upwards by the coolness of the green.
And here, stuck in a fork, he came across
A jackdaw's nest. It was not as tidy
As his neat cup, nor as comfortable -
A mass of sticks was roughly lined with wool.
Curious, Spad perched above, head cocked,
And gazed in. Some interesting insects
Crawled over bits of glass and shining things
Half'-hidden in the base

                Spad felt a need
For food, but as he landed on the side
And poised to strike, he heard a warning 'Caw'!
Deep and disapproving. He heard wings flap

But thought he had the time to make his kill
And still escape. He bent to aim and strike
Just as the owner came, and as the shadow
Loomed, he pecked and missed, put off by that dark
Presence, and picked up a piece of glass!

He did not know - how could he? - that of all
The treasures stored and counted in the nest
The little sliver settled in his beak
Was nearest, dearest to the jackdaw's heart.
Spad fled! The jackdaw, with an outraged roar,
Leapt to pursue!
      How fast Spad flew, the jewel
In his beak! And, curious to relate,
The greater speed he made, the faster
It was wedged.
     Out of the woods he galloped,
Not caring where he went, his one intention
To leave the irate jackdaw far behind.
Into the blazing heat and over fields
He went, his chaser flapping angrily
And shouting out with rage.
      Some instinct sent
Spad home. Too late, he recognised. the field
Now sweeping into view, peopled with his
Would-be murderers! But where to go now?
The cries across the field were those of foes;
The cries behind of obdurate enmity.
It was as though he'd carefully laid a trap
And sprung it on himself!
      Up! Up! he urged.

But too late! The starlings now were massing
To attack; the jackdaw lunged and just missed
In his strike.
              Now, over his own home, Spad,
Almost out of breath, gasped and opened wide
His beak. Out fell the glass, tumbling, spinning,
Flashing in the light.
                  The lorn jackdaw wailed
And dropped to follow - but was beaten back
By the rising mob of bitter starlings.
Spad circled slowly, waiting for his end.
The little piece of glass was drifting down,
And as it went, it gathered threads of light,
And as it turned, it span them into cords,
And these in turn it twisted all together,
So when it reached the nadir of its flight,
It held a rope of sunlight coiled within
Which was unleashed in all its burning force!
From where it landed came a little smoke.
A little breeze then fanned it into flame.
The little flame grew stronger and the breeze
Grew stronger too. A meadow flower, straight
Among the grass, then swayed violently,
Danced, before bursting spontaneously
Into fire, the whole at once, the yellow
Petals twisting, melting, crumpling, charring,
While the roots smouldered underground.
And then,
Faster than a hare can run; more rapid
Than a rabbit's fastest thought; more quickly

Than a falcon's stoop; in one reaction,
Like the lightning strike of an uncoiling
And contentious snake, living flames leapt
Right across the field, flooding the hollows,
Scaling tussocks, thistles, plantains, shrubs,
Transforming every tree into a torch
And roaring down the crannies of the hedge.
The smell came first and then the searing heat,
And then the choking fumes, white smoke pouring
                                            up,
All but screening the vivid crimson edging
Of the fire. Then a mighty rushing wind
Lifted the flames for twenty- thirty- more-
Feet in the air. Like a wounded predator
The fire clawed at the sky until, exhausted,
It fell into a smouldering, sulky waste.
And thus a generation was expunged!
Alas! Alas! for ruined starlingdom!
The terror of the flames engulfed them all.
They lay in blackened heaps across the field,
Scattered where they fell, murdered by the fumes
And singeing in the ash. And all for being
Good at being starlings!
                      And what of Spad?
The heat was so intense he nearly fainted.
But then the smell of slowly charring feathers
Brought him round, and he had strength enough
To flutter to a wholesome branch to breathe.

As for the jackdaw, he went sadly home,
His eyes watering, his feet hot, mourning
The treasure which he had lost for ever;
An innocent observer, sadly mauled

(VIII)

Aftermath

As if to mark such a tumultuous time,
Enormous clouds came racing overhead,
Flat-headed, anvil-shaped and ominous.
The world darkened; the steam and idling ashes,
Trapped beneath the lowering vapours, thickened,
Heated, swirled and poisoned the purer air,
Until there seemed no possibility
Of breathing steadily. Like a noxious tide
Spreading into some foul and stinking creek.
The reek lapped steadily across the land.
No place was safe. no twig, no perch, no hole,
No blackened branch, no scorched and brittle nest-
All were marked down and swallowed, all taken.
What few survivors lived - a rabbit ringed
With ashes on her deathbed; a shouting dove
Now silenced to a whimper; two vipers
In a thorn, twined round the topmost branches
Skins blistered; and some several finches,
Fire blasted, wind scorched, with crippled
                                      feathers
And burnt faces - all fought for breath, all gasped
For air, all thought their pounding hearts would
                                      burst.
And as they gazed across the smouldering waste
And saw the twisting curls of intermittent
Smoke, the little shoots of red, the shimmer

In the air above the cinders, it seemed
As though the piles of charring starling dead
Were stirring, shifting. breathing out the fumes;
Enough for these poor wretches to surmise
What their own end would be, how it would come.

Interminable and intolerable
Was the waiting underneath that sky.
The clouds massed higher, pressed lower,
And all the land grew sombre, still and tense.
Nothing moved; nothing sounded; hope had gone.
And then there came a leaping puff of dust,
Ashes and steam combined. Soon there were more,
Accompanied by drumming on the earth,
And then the field was spattered by huge drops.
The sky turned black before there came a flash,
A bolt of lightning, blue and shimmering white,
Which struck old Owl's old tree and blazed it forth,
Electrified in each particular
Like some strange symbol of a cruel clan,
Standing out against the panorama
Of the dark.   It faded, leaving etchings
On the mind and excited thoughts of doom.
Colder now, the rain halted and the air
                              shivered.
When the explosion came, it stunned
By its proximity and volume, numbed
By the liberation of such potent
And irresponsible forces. There was
No time to flinch and there was no action

Possible, save to endure the dreadful
Battering of the senses.
                              It rolled away
Across the wasted pasture as a prelude
To the tempest, for next the rains came down,
Not in the steady deluge of a storm,
But in the frenzied fury of a madman.
It seemed there was an ocean up above
All fighting to descend at once. No eye
Could separate the drops. No flesh could stand
Such constant hammering. To be exposed
But for a moment was to risk immersion.
The earth was hard, baked and impermeable
And in a trice it was an inland sea,
Awash with rippling wavelets, lashed by rain,
Spreading through furrows, swamping in the
                                        hedge.
As lightning flashes lit the hectic scene,
So those who blinked at each disjunctive strike
Must have seen much of what old Noah viewed-
A world well-flooded, storm-tossed, desolate,
A choppy watery waste which drowned a land
Corrupt. And as the waters moved, seeking
Their level, so did the corpses balance
On the tide, shift like beds of seaweed,
Float to and fro like some polluting agent,
What had been local and particular
Becoming general, so that disease
Would gently spread its influence everywhere.

(IX)

Spad Alone

So Spad lay resting in that waiting time
And suffered torment in the lightning flash
And following explosion overhead.
At first he thought it was his death, that he'd
Been torn apart and thus distributed
In pieces round the field. He fainted,
Fell headfirst, and fluttered to the ground.

                              Rain
Revived him, hissing to his aching joints
And fuddled head with penetrating aim.
Soon it was too much for him to suffer:
His feathers would be soaked, too water-logged
To lift; he would be grounded, cold, unsafe.
Besides, his chin was resting in a dip
Where water was collecting at a speed
Which filled him with alarm. He must escape!
He struggled to his feet and made to fly,
But could not! He found his near-side wing
Was paralysed and quite unfit for use;
Jammed open, it was trailing on the ground.
Numb at the tip and throbbing at the shoulder,
The pain increased the more he thought of it.

By now the rain was tippling, streaming down,
An aerial bombardment so intense

That each drop was bounced upwards to the clouds
Before it fell again. And in this way
The fury of the storm was suffered twice.

Spad's courage was so battered by the rain
That lying down and dying crossed his mind;
Drowning, he thought, would be an easy way.
And soon would be no option, for the flood
Was rising rapidly beneath his beak.
The coldness of the water numbed his pain;
His legs appeared to work, but very stiff
And lacking power. Yet he could travel
If only at a crippled, halting pace.
Therefore, without commanding from his brain,
He hopped towards a little nearby hillock
And so attempted thus to save himself.

When he perceived the waters rising fast
And analysed his own predicament
Then was he near to giving up again.
Yet, as he blinked the water from his eyes,
He saw the perch from which he had just come
Within an easy reach - had he been strong.
And there beneath it was an eminence,
Above the flood, beneath a blackened branch,
Which gave some little prospect of respite
From the storm and its effects.

                        To get there
Now became his aim. And yet the rain, alas!
Was doubled, trebled in its stark intensity

That now a wind was driving it aslant.

A mist arose above the swimming torrents;
Spad found it hard to see and even breathe.
And yet, if he would live, he must attempt
The crossing! To linger would mean drowning.

In fearful mood, with frightened, tiny steps
He dragged down to the water's edge and stopped,
For it was swirling, dirty, violent,
With creamy froth and bubbles in the brown.
He held his head up high and closed his eyes
And took one nervous step. The water surged
And plucked him from the land, out of his depth,
And, like a whirlpool, span him round and round.
Blind and half-suffocated, Spad had sense
Enough to hold his injured wing aloft,
Out of the flood, to try and keep it safe.
And so he floated like a fallen leaf,
Fast filling up with water, helpless, mute.

And then the wind made matters worse! It caught
His outstretched wing, which wavered in between
The sea and sky like an old Arab sail,
Beaten in all directions by the storm.
Pity poor Spad! The waters race one way,
The wind would blow them back upon themselves,
And in the middle sinks our little dunnock,
Water-logged and helpless.
                          But then his toes,
Reaching through the swirls, felt a stem of grass

And wrapped themselves around it. Thus anchored
He hung motionless until a greater
Gust of wind pulled at his feathers, drove him
Against the tide. caused him to pluck his stalk
Clean from the mud, and dumped him in the
                                 shallows
By the hedge. He crawled ashore, like Crusoe
From his storm, aching for rest.
                           So Spad lay,
Panting, oozing water, sick, cold and chilling,
Plastered with mud and blinded by the silt,
His mouth half-full of filth he dare not name,
His wounded wing more battered by the storm
And trailing uselessly. And yet, between
His toes he clutched a straw, and in its end
There was one tiny seed, which seemed to hint
That desperate although his state might be,
There could be hope for better times to come.

(X)

Exile

Now began Spad's miserable time,
A time when he would need each small resource
Of strength and energy, of pride and skill.
Domestic, his sweet nest had been destroyed;
A bird who ranged along a territory,
His patch was burnt and flooded, nullified;

A bird who needed company, support,
Now found himself alone, friendless, bereft
Of any warmth or thing he recognised
As making life worthwhile. There was his self
And nothing interposed which gave protection
From this cold, heartless, neutral universe.
There was no place to go but far away:
And so he left, crawling, limping, weeping,
Trailing his damaged wing through mud and stones,
Convinced that he would never hop that way
Again, never be healthy. never feel
The sun's rays warm upon his back, never
Be happy; forever doomed to wander,
Lonely in an alien countryside.

And then there was the rain! It fell unceasing
From leaking clouds which drifted low and full,
Until the world was saturated through.
Sodden like the basement of a mere,
With all the prospect of a harvest ruined!

Three weeks the unremitting rain came down
And brought rot with it. Spad was never dry;
Never warm; always hungry; always in pain.
No matter where he crept, in fields or hedges,
By walls or gardens, under foreign trees,
Under the eaves of barns or cattle pens,
Anywhere where he might peck a mouthful,
A rotting seed or just a dying grub
Which might perhaps alleviate his hurts,
There was he then the one to be expelled,

The stranger to be driven off, outsider
To be harried, hustled, chased and killed.

Gamekeeper turned poacher, Spad found skills
Of sneaking theft. He learned to hide in shadows,
Lie up unmoving in a noisome spot,
Wait for the owners to desert a meal
And then move in to take the leavings.
But many a time the table was quite bare
Or what was left was nothing fit to eat,
So he went hungry, aching in the night.
And yet he made a living of a sort
With just enough to keep himself alert.

He was much thinner when the rains left off.
That night, he'd been in luck, for he had found
A pigeon loft, and scattered on the ground
Was straw and in amongst it were good seeds,
Wholesome and dry and just the sort of thing
To set a Dunnock up. Unwatched, he gorged,
And, feeling better, dragged his trailing wing
Across the darker patches of the yard
Into the shelter of a mulberry tree.

And then he realised there was a moon
And all the world was steaming after rain.
He peered upward with a wondering eye
At so much brilliance and a clear sky.
He recognised the pattern of the stars
And drew some comfort from a heavenly show
Which was not strange. He shuffled on his branch

Until he was quite hidden by the twigs
And safe from moonlight. Tired by the strain
Of being brave, he tucked his aching head
Beneath his one sound wing and fell asleep.

When he awoke, the world had changed again.
Gone was the wind, the softness brought by rain,
The light diffused and spread by heavy clouds -
Instead the place was fashioned by the sun,
Lit brilliantly from the east, with long shadows
Hurtful to the eyes, and all was silent,
Listening.
              Spad jerked awake in sudden fear!
He wondered what was wrong, what different?
And then the understanding came: his feet
Were frozen, almost glued, by quick-formed ice
And all his tree was furred and edged with frost!
And it was cold! Heart-stopping in its power!
He freed his feet and looked out at a scene
Transformed: whispers ran like shouts; neighbour
                                         trees
Hung motionless in white, their glazed branches
Shining in the sun; the leaves of hedges
Were new-made flowers which blossomed once again
In overall and delicate profusion.

There was no beauty here for Spad. He saw
The superficial shine, the light which flooded
Coldness everywhere, Nature clean and pure,
Was but another burden to be borne: -
Worse than a burden, an icy dagger

Pointed at his heart! His case was over:
He had been considered and a judgement made;
His sentence had been passed without the hope
Of any clemency; now he must die
In lingering battles with his will to live
Which all the time he knew that he must lose.

What food was there in this? What kind of shelter
That could sustain him, weakened as he was?
No, his future was as plain as any truth:
Either to die of cold and lie quite stiff,
A fan of quills unqualified by flesh,
Preserved 'til sexton beetles came in Spring;
Or elevate his throat to some hot killer,
The weasel's fury or the fox's grin,
And leave a transient rouge upon the ice.

As if to reinforce these morbid thoughts,
A rangy farmyard cat stepped daintily
Upon the path which Spad had dragged last night.
She stopped and lifted up her nose to taste
The morning air. Her eyes were merely slits
Of concentration. Spad kept very still.
She stood so, with her tail slowly waving,
Her ears pricked, whiskers forward, one paw
                                      raised -
Then she bent her head to sniff the gravel
And lashed her tall in violent display
Of temper. She looked around and sniffed again
And cried aloud. But then her eye was caught
And held as a pigeon landed nearbye
And waddled, neck jerking, quite unafraid,

Right up to her. Another came and more,
And yet more, all busy taking pebbles
From the ground. She turned languidly away
As though that place could hold no interest
For her, and sauntered elegantly off
Because she had some business otherwhere.

Spad knew that he must go. She would be back
In time more promising. Laboriously
He shuffled off, hoping to find a mouthful
On the way. He took the hidden passages
And was not troubled any more that day.

(X1)

Winter

Then nature turned her hard and cruel side
Toward the kind who struggled in her lap,
And what she had donated, took away.
Spad woke into a winter deep in snow,
Dull white and gleaming under leaden skies,
Britain was smothered, plain and moor and hill,
Bleached and blanched within the icy sea.
Nor was it any mere aberrant act,
For full five months the isle was frozen deep,
With blizzards, snowstorms, murderous icicles
Which played wild tunes upon the savage winds.

What damage now was done as night closed in!
Rocks fractured by the ice and hills reshaped;
Rivers still and motionless, suspended;
Great venerable trees broken like toys,
Wormed by ice and crumpled under snow,
Limbs lopped off, the very heart-wood riven
By the slow and deadly lightning of the cold.
And then the fox was barking at the moon,
A hollow sound across the desolate waste.

And in the morning, what a fearful sight!
The wind of death had breathed across the land:
Birds lay in thousands, frozen where they slept;
Rabbits had suffocated underground;
Elvers were frozen solid in the mud
And foxes pawed the snow in desperation,
Thinking to start a beetle or a mouse;
Weasels, hoping for a taste of blood, ploughed
Into drifts and perished in their depths;
Crows and rooks were seeking out the dead,
Black shadows twisting in the shallow sun,
Their harsh cries sounding from the icy hills
And shattering the sullen, throttled quiet.

So how should Spad survive where others fell?
Perhaps his frame was stronger than it looked,
Or that his will to win was firmer fixed,
Or that his instinct took him always on
When danger threatened, so that he escaped
Into the lee, the less severe side.

However be it, he did yet live on,
If eating snow and clawing frost-burnt branches
For withered fruit and yellow tissue leaves
Which might contain a little nourishment;
If always being frightened, cold perpetually,
Knowing he left a trail behind him in the snow
Which any predator might recognise
And follow for the kill: if this was living
Then Spad was still alive. At times, he thought,
The only one. And all the time the nights
Were growing longer, colder, more intense.

So picture our young hero on a day
When there was feeble sunshine. There he is
Struggling in the bottom of a hedge.
He is counting now his strength, like a miser
Who is forced to spend his golden pennies,
To find the strength to save the few remaining
Near the drain hole in the floor. Spad equals
Almost nought. The fuel tank is empty;
The spirits low and lowering.   Think then
Of his despair when coming to a corner
Where his hedge met another at an angle
Beneath a splintered, whitened willow tree,
He was confronted by the spreading paws
The delicate black stockings, whirling brush
And slant-eyed grinning rictus of a fox!
He was appalled to see that dripping tongue
Rippling in between the yellow teeth,

And nearly fainted at the gust of eager breath.
He reared back, his instincts to escape
Started by that visage. He tried to fly
By flapping both his wings and left the ground
By inches, drifting back. Although quite weak,
His damaged wing would work. He drew once
                                            more
On his resources, stood up and flapped them both
In frantic pain and general despair.

And at the very moment when the fox,
Head on one side, had just prepared to snap,
One paw uplifted for a blow,
A little mouse was startled by Spad's wings
And ran it knew not where across the snow
Between the two of them. The fox, distracted,
Paused, and in that time a young tawny owl
Swept in and snatched the tiny, squeaking thing.
The fox leapt and pawed the air, but too late,
The owl was sitting safe upon a branch,
The long tall hanging wriggling from his beak.

Spad, in the lower branches of the hedge,
Climbed higher, rested, and kept very still.
The tail vanished in one convulsive gulp.
The owl looked down upon the leaping fox
And blinked his huge eyes twice. He flapped his
                                            wings
And swallowed before hissing down at him,
When with a sudden movement he came out,

Floating on silent wings and skimmed the ground,
Aiming, it seemed, straight for the panting jaws.
Just like a feather wafting in the heat
Which rises in a column from a fire
Smoking on the forest floor, turning round,
Sliding sideways or dancing quickly up,
Fluttering, perhaps helplessly, so Owl
Shifted over and around the snarling fox,
Playing with fire! And how the creature tried
To catch the drifting bird: falling over,
Boxing at the air with probing forepaws.
And all the time not noticing that inch by inch
He was being led into the middle
Of a field and then from that, far away
Into a strip of wood beyond a hedge.

Spad watched them go and felt a deep relief.

He climbed a little higher up his hedge,
And once up there, he tried his damaged wing.
He found that he could move it painfully
And slowly. It was weak and limp and sore
But he could make it work. He exercised,
Extending and flapping, stretching and turning,
Something he hadn't done since in the nest
He first learned to fly.
                        Resting, he looked up,
And, with a shock, he saw that Owl was back,
Sitting on a stump not five feet off
And staring at him with his glowing eyes.
Spad had not heard him come!

                    He looked away,
Unwilling to submit. Yet something pulled,
Making his eyes come back to search that face.

Now Owls can't smile and neither could Spad talk,
So in what way could they communicate?
Well, who can say but that a common misery
Brought uppermost community of interest?
That feather spoke to feather, nerve to nerve;
Claws hooked in harmony and sinews in accord;
Blood pulsed in sympathy, each breath proclaimed
A need of mutual help.
                            Spad knew that Owl
Impressive though he was, was wandering,
Lonely, homeless like himself, scratching food
Where he could in someone else's territory,
That he had been mobbed away by parents
Or by siblings stronger than himself.
And Owl would have been blind to have ignored
The state of Spad's weak wing and general
Condition of his health and fortitude.
With what remained of winter yet to come
The chances each would have of living on
Into the luxury of summer's plenty
Were slim indeed. But if they could combine,
Sustain a pact, subdue their independence,
They might survive as pair, whereas singly
They would surely perish.
                            Owl began it.
He made a little noise deep in his throat
And spread his wings and floated softly off,

Gliding across the field to that same hedge
Where he had snared the fox in foolishness.
Once there, he hooted gently over the snow.
Spad climbed the topmost branches of his shrub.
He knew he was to follow if he could;
He spread his wings and moved them up and down.

He was built for flying, not for gliding;
He could not soar, he had to flap for flight.
So could he do it? It was so far away
And he was weak and crippled with the pain.
Yet, like a learner in a swimming pool,
Who sees the side which he must reach, or sink
In ignominy, so Spad raised his chest
And beat his wings and aimed him for the mark.
Pride drove him on - and nearly burst his lungs
And caused such agony that once he thought
His wings were ripped out at the very roots
And he would lie with creeping things forever.
And yet he made it, just, and fluttered
To the bottom of the hedge, too blind to see
Why Owl had called him there.
      When he recovered,
He saw a little dimple in the snow,
Some trick of wind had left the ground quite bare,
And sprouting in the patch some rattling weeds.
And on them and around them on the earth
Were seeds, a treasure trove for Spad to eat.

When the last one was pecked and pouched, the ground
Searched two or three times more in case of one

Which might have been mislaid, Spad felt new life
Suffusing all his veins. He looked at Owl
And took his meaning in the full. He, too,
Would play his part, and with the promise came
A welcome, tiny finger-end of warmth.

(XII)

Partner

And still it snowed and still it froze and blew
Almost without remit. Nights were foulest,
With howling gales screaming over ice-falls
And dangerous from fractured, falling branches,
From toppling trees, from driving, blinding snow,
From temperatures too low to be inhaled.
The days were short and drab, monotonous
In cold and damp, preoccupied with food
And keeping warm and plodding on, hoping
That life could still continue through the day,
Survive the night, and yet be warm the morrow.
Which Spad and Owl had now some hope of
                                        doing.
For Spad could fly a little more each day,
And with each increment derived more hope,
Now he could forage more effectively,
And consequently gather yet more strength.
And this helped Owl, for they could hunt together.

They learned the practice by an accident:
It came that Spad was flying down a hedge.

Looking for any spike of grass or weed
　　Which stuck up through the snow when suddenly
　　His quiet rush of wings surprised a mouse
　　Which ran from his approach into the claws
　　　　　　　　　　　Of watching owl.

Spad turned his eyes away from that grim feast
And looked down at the claw marks in the snow
Made by that mouse which even now was wriggling
To its end inside owl's stomach. He saw
What that dead creature had been working at -
Scratching the snow in search of seeds -
And flew down to investigate the scrapes.
There was enough to give him half a meal
And so he pecked away quite vigorously,
While Owl sat ruminating on a gate,
Eyes closed and passive, stately and content.
So Spad became a beater for the Owl,
Flushing out voles and shrews and, once, a rat
　Which Owl could kill but could not quite devour.
　By chance there was a baby in her nest,
　And that sufficed.
　　　　　　　　　And as for hungry Spad,
With what he found of stores along the way,
Under the lee of barns, of dregs not taken
By domestic fowl, of husks of pigeon food,
Of tit-blts spread for cottage garden birds,
He made enough to keep his fires alight.

One night they found an empty Squirrel's drey
Beyond the first fork of a dying beech.

The sky was clear, the air was very cold
And Spad sat out along the branch to watch
The night come in. Truth to tell, he was afraid
To snuggle up to Owl in that dark hole,
For he was not much bigger than the prey
Which Owl could swallow up in one huge gulp.
Nor had Owl eaten for a day or two.
And so he shivered in the open air
And listened to the Owl as he reorganised
The stuff the squirrel used to warm himself.

The sun was crimson, glowing, cold: the fields
Of snow were burning in that light; overhead
The sky was dark with one or two bright stars
Twinkling bravely; some few trees held their
                                    boughs
Like black markers across the dying furnace
In the west, pointing to the past; the air,
The ground, the tree, were creaking with the onset
Of the cold. And out of this, Spad picked
A little stir of hope. Healing had started.
He knew it in his bones and in his heart.
Somewhat cheered, he hopped upon the threshold
And looked in. Owl lifted one large eyelid
And Spad knew that he knew what he had feared.
He had not known that owls could laugh, but his
Was laughing now, so Spad jumped in and sat
Heavily beside the bigger bird, chirped,
And, as the warmth began to penetrate,
Closed his eyes and tumbled into sleep

XIII

Home

So for a little time they lived in warmth
And each enjoyed the new-found company
In the ragged drey; but all too quickly
They had to move in search of food.
                                          Onward,
Across the desolate countryside, they
Flew and hopped and hunted, the truce still held
Quite firm. The light had altered; there was more
Each day and, responsive to each subtle change,
They felt a corresponding lightening
Of their hearts.
                              Now Owl was rootless, exiled:
It were possible, had he not met Spad,
He would have perished in the heavy snow,
Not from lack of food but lack of loving.
Spad, on the other hand, despite his nous,
Was homesick. He yearned for his natal field,
His flowering hedge, its greenery and all
The wealth and glory of its insect life.

And as time passed, he found the Owl to be
Something of a burden. He had to work
For both, find food for both. And so he did
What many young men do when landed with
A slow, demanding friend - he took him home.

How Spad was so cognisant of the route -
Well, who can tell? The fact is that he was,
And further, that his navigational
Skills were steady, even without recourse
To star or compass, swinging moon or sun.
Nostalgia was the cloud which led him on
Through the day, memories of the fire which
                                        burned
Within his dreams each night.

                         Unerringly,
The course was taken by the straightest route,
Until one day he looked upon the field again
With such a shock of sweet and old surprise,
With such a sense of pain at what he found -
Coming upon it, as he did, much sooner
Than he had hoped, he nearly passed it by -
That Spad could only stare across the space
And note the sheet of ice, the blackened stumps,
The terrifying scorch marks still preserved
In frost - and feel himself a fool!
                               And at his side,
Owl breathed deeply in his chest and wondered
At the place and what Spad's reasoning
Could be, to halt in such a barren hedge.
And yet, like some old cunning warrior king,
Who would surprise his enemy, and thus
Gathers his silent forces in the hills,
In gullies, ravines, copses, valley sides,

Collecting quiet strength, then so, above
The clouds, behind the wind, beyond the snow,
The old sun had been hopping ever north,
Grandmother's steps, unnoticed down on earth.
This was his moment and he chose it well:
The clouds unfolded at his golden touch
And all the field was flooded with his warmth.
Spad closed his eyes against the light, and when
He blinked them wide, he saw to his great joy,
A spray of frenzied winter gnats, dancing
Above the ice. Fresh meat! He leapt to eat.
And what a pleasure was it now to catch
The sun-drugged things! How sweet to swoop and
                                          swirl
In gentle, failing warmth!
                            When he had taken
All he could, he swept joyfully around
His own, old field, just for the sheer pleasure
Of flying it again. Now up; now down;
High from hedge to hedge: and then a swooping
Fast, low pass.
                And it was then he saw a thing
Which filled his heart with hope. Beneath the ice
Which stretched across the field like glass across
A picture, he perceived the burnt remains
Of pastures which he had himself destroyed
The previous year. But in amongst the blackened,
Brittle stalks, just showing tiny headings,
Tender, like the little horns of snails,
And misty in that shimmering translucence,
As though their breath was painted on the glass.

Were pale green shootlets, just about to come.

Back in the hedge, where Owl was suffering
With tight shut eyes, he found more evidence.
Beneath the coat of soot, what he had thought
Of as dead sticks, had reddened, were suffused,
Flushed pale with intimations of new growth.
And all along the twigs were adventitious
Swellings. It seemed as though the earth beneath
Was stirring, shaking free its furry coat,
Ready for fresh work.
                     And all of it was his!

Suddenly he found a need to be alone,
To not to have to share. to keep it private.
And here was Owl's great bulk, over-looming
His pleasure! He watched him raise one eye-lid
Just enough to peer out and then slam it shut,
While a tear formed in the corner. Time now
To place him. He whistled low and set off
For the old oak in the coppice by the stream.
And it was there! The old tree, scarred and
                                 scorched
But still standing, still alive and shining
In the sun. He showed his friend where old Owl
Used to stand and where he rested. Owl seemed
To understand. He sniffed and huffed and hooted
Softly and at that particular moment
Began to grow, mature before Spad's eyes.
He was taller, stiffer, more commanding;
Magisterial in his demeanour.

His very gait was altered in its style.
With what dignity he strutted sideways
On his branch, his neck twisting in all ways
As he surveyed his new domain! With what
Lordly interest he pried and peered
Into his new living quarters! And then,
How gravely he dismissed Spad, so that he
Could go about his own small affairs!

                              Spad
Took the hint and flew back home rejoicing.

XIV

Finale

The snow had melted and the floods had gone:
The sun was rising higher day by day
And life was buzzing in and round the field.
Spad perched upon his favourite, springing twig
Now well past leafing and come into bloom,
And crawling with his own particular food.
He felt the welcome heat upon his back
And sweet contentment crooning through his veins;
He closed his eyes in bliss and thankfulness
His bones were dry and warm and serviceable.

Now was the time to nod off in the sun,
To take a little nap as his reward,

Surrounded as he was by all the din
Of Nature's wantoness and procreation.
He closed his eyes into a warm, red dark
And felt a little trickle down his wing
Some way between a tickle and a thrill -
But most acceptable!
                          He thought at first
The sun was teasing out the final knots
Of his recovered wing, until it came again,
A firmer stitching down the seam between
His wing and body; a knocking, were it
Not ridiculous to say so, at a door,
A tapping to be let in, the whole phase
Ending with a definite caress.

It stopped and Spad woke up immediately
And there, near to him, with her head haloed
By the sun, a dunnock in the gleam of health
And youth, was looking at him most demandingly.
She was not coy, but met his gaze directly,
And held it for a moment, before stretching out
Her neck to touch his wing root, like a thread
Which drifts aslant, trapped in a summer wind.
But it could have been a hammer in the ribs
For what effect it had! The beak completed
What the frank and friendly eyes began.
Spad stared at her as possibilities
Opened before him, like shouted echoes
Reverberating through expanding caves
Of mirrored surfaces.
                      She ducked her head

And sidled down the branch until she stood
There, firmly at his side, and he could feel
The steady, rapid beating of her heart.
And Spad knew what to do! He leant to nibble
At the feathers on her neck, and her pleasure
Rose with his.
        Claimed, he sprang from the twig
And brought her back a juicy insect grub
And fed it to her. Thus consolidated,
They promenaded through the sunlit hedge,
Twittering incessantly, momently
More certain in each other's company:
A battle-hardened Dunnock and his Maid!

That night they roosted on Spad's favourite
                              branch,
Snuggled together. Spad could not catch sleep:
He listened to the distant nightingale
And heard Owl hissing love songs to his mate
On the old oak. He looked up, wondering,
At the oceans of the sky, where stars drifted
In huge banks and silver shoals, and pondered
The broad, denuded belly of the moon,
So friendly now, and thought about the past.
And then he laughed inside with joy and triumph;
For he was Spad and he had just come through,
And life was sweet to taste upon the tongue.
His new mate stirred and preened him with her beak
And that was almost more than he could bear!

And if he heard an echo from the past

Of Spadgette's soft, 'Let's do it all again',
He kept it to himself. For now, it seemed,
That there would be a clutch of little Spads
To hop and hunt along the hedge and field,
As Spads had always done. And that would be
His glory, to have made it possible.

He gave up thinking, shut his eyes and slept,
But not before his mate responded true.

EVERYWHERE I LOOK

(from Mumchance)

Every where I look, I see
Things which are outliving me:
Aqueducts and railway arches,
Apple trees and sapling larches,
Old canals, their locks and bridges,
Stone walls, hedges lining ridges,
Roman roads and mountain passes,
All the sweet and poisonous gases -
Even things I have forgot
Will be here when I am not.

Everything I am will go,
All my pleasure, all my woe,
My small talents, my great dreams,
Hopes and fears and stifled screams,
All my oaths, my marriage vows,
My hates, my friendships, lusts and rows,
My little wisdom, huge ideas,
Knowledge, folly, untruths, fears -
Even things I have forgot
Will have gone when I am not.

        Septimus Shrabcock
        (1890-1970)

So, seekers, let your verdict be
He tried to live in harmony;
Let tolerance and justice stand
For his philosophic brand,
With mercy, gratitude and love
As his passport to above.
I, his son, inscribed this stone
With all the love for which he's known
Just so he will not be forgot
When all the things he was are not.

      Clive Shrabcock
       (1971)

Index of First Lines

	Page
A man who has faced death remains afraid	36
A pale watery gleam glows through the mist	101
A rumour ran along the hedges, passed	122
All human thought is here and hope and love	90
Although my anger's gone and my wild outrage	69
And still it snowed and still it froze and blew	162
As a fold or crinkle in magnetic tape	59
As if to mark such a tumultuous time	144
Behind me lies the bright side	98
Cold winter sunlight floods the room. I sit	44
Everywhere I look, I see	173
First thoughts are no	74
Footprints, footprints	13
For that which is honest, simple and true	9
For who can say which way his mind should turn?	39
Foucault perceived it	95
Her accent was pure	89
Here, Now, Today	30
His huge figure dominates the clearing	23
How sweet it is to draw a deep	56
I am no scientist	84
I first came here some thirty years ago	26
I hardly knew my father, never knew	35
I took the bricks and placed them on the ground	83
If there is one thing which is certain about grass	18
In late autumn, after the bronze time	20
In South America	80
In the classroom, they are planning a painting	107
In this corner of a draughty land	63
It is a truth niversally knowledged	96

It was a strange holiday in the end	48
It's true my hair is now more grey than black	42
It was all new to him	62
Let us imagine the death of a great pianist	85
Marvell said music was mosaic	81
Midwinter and the armed man comes	11
Never looking, always peeping	74
Next day they came again.	131
No plastic smiles	106
No post again today and none, I guess	102
No rain had fallen now for many weeks	126
No! I don't care! That's how feel today!	100
No. Thirty-nine is not a proper number	110
Now began Spad's miserable time	150
Of course you know there's nothing in my mind	73
Old men revisit places where	97
On Friday, the factory where I worked	77
Once they have died and, safely, can't reply	99
Outside my window lies an urgent world	80
Said he	77
She had the longest length of fetch I've seen	38
Sleep, my little conscience, sleep	72
Small men and virile	15
So for a little time they lived in warmth	165
So much vitality! And is it all	37
So Spad lay resting in that waiting time	147
So Spad sat glooming, crouched upon a branch	115
That night he slept in better health, replete	137
That time, the summer of the blistering drought	65
That year, warm rain was early	111
The household cat sits straight	77
The morning sun contains a touch of gold	45
The music pumping through my head	108
The panther stirred	64

The room is dim and cold.	84
The scene is simple, windswept	59
The snow had melted and the floods had gone	169
The summer ripened and the nestlings grew	119
Then nature turned her hard and cruel side	146
There was a date	87
There was no plan: no genius laid down	60
Those women who will weep their way	40
Thoughts felt, sensations veined and dark	54
Today I want to give a toast	57
Waiting	31
We have seen a maddened people as they strut	92
What will happen to your knowledge	54
When I remember Seasides, I don't see	71
When I sleep with the windows open	78
When I was young	76
When I was young, I sat in class	81
When we abandoned the horse	46
When we follow a path to the place	25
Who am I to ask for pleasure	56
Who can deny the claim she made her mind?	41
Who dares to say I've seen my better times?	43
With what passion when we meet	68
With what steep steps we lurch along the way	104
Yes, I was there that night. I saw	47
Yes, I'm an academic; I love books	103
Yet when it came, it came with ease.	105

www.ingramcontent.com/pod-product-compliance
Lightning Source LLC
Chambersburg PA
CBHW051756040426
42446CB00007B/396